A NEW QUEST
OF THE HISTORICAL JESUS

by the same author
THE PROBLEM OF HISTORY IN MARK

A NEW QUEST
OF THE
HISTORICAL JESUS

JAMES M. ROBINSON

Professor of Theology and New Testament
Southern California School of Theology
Claremont

SCM PRESS LTD
BLOOMSBURY STREET LONDON

SBN 334 01122 1

First published 1959
Second impression 1961
Third impression 1963
Fourth impression 1966
Fifth impression 1968

Printed in Great Britain
by Photolithography
Unwin Brothers Limited
Woking and London

CONTENTS

Contents

LIST OF ABBREVIATIONS

BZ, n.F.	*Biblische Zeitschrift,* neue Folge
ChrW	*Die Christliche Welt*
EvTh	*Evangelische Theologie*
ExpT	*The Expository Times*
GuV	Rudolf Bultmann, *Glauben und Verstehen,* Vol. I, 1933. (Vol. II, 1952, is cited from the Engl tr., *Essays Philosophical and Theological,* 1955.)
JBL	*Journal of Biblical Literature*
JTS, n.s.	*Journal of Theological Studies,* new series
KD	Karl Barth, *Kirchliche Dogmatik,* 1932 ff.
KuD	*Kerygma und Dogma*
KuM	*Kerygma und Mythos,* ed. II. W. Bartsch, 1948–55
RGG	*Die Religion in Geschichte und Gegenwart*
SgV	*Sammlung gemeinverständlicher Vorträge*
STK	*Svensk Teologisk Kvartalskrift*
TB	*Theologische Blätter*
TLZ	*Theologische Literaturzeitung*
TR, n.F.	*Theologische Rundschau,* neue Folge
TZ	*Theologische Zeitschrift*
TWNT	*Theologisches Wörterbuch zum Neuen Testament*
VuF	*Verkündigung und Forschung*
ZNTW	*Zeitschrift für die neutestamentliche Wissenschaft*
ZTK	*Zeitschrift für Theologie und Kirche*

I

INTRODUCTION

A. THE 'BULTMANNIAN' EPOCH IN GERMAN THEOLOGY

The present work is intended as a programmatic essay, i.e. as a contribution to basic thought about the unfulfilled task of New Testament scholarship. Hence its point of departure is not in the relatively untroubled and uninterrupted quest of the historical Jesus going on in French[1] and Anglo-Saxon[2] scholarship. Rather it is based upon the conviction that this continuation of the nineteenth-century German quest ought probably to be interrupted or at least disturbed. The present study has to do with a

[1] The standard treatment of the quest since Schweitzer is Maurice Goguel's 'Histoire des vies de Jésus', Ch. I of his *Jésus*, 1950, which is the 2nd ed. of his *Vie de Jésus*, 1932. This and the *Jésus* of Charles Guignebert, 1933, both available in English, are the most significant French biographies. The French quest has been traced by Jean C. H. Hoffmann, *Les vies de Jésus et le Jésus de l'histoire*, 1947.

[2] Cf. the long bibliography of American lives of Christ made available by Otto A. Piper, 'Das Problem des Lebens Jesu seit Schweitzer', *Verbum Dei manet in aeternum*, 1953, 73–93. Cf. also C. C. McCown, *The Search for the Real Jesus; a Century of Historical Study*, 1940. Typical of the British monographs treating the problem are : R. H. Strachan, *The Historical Jesus in the New Testament*, 1931; E. C. Hoskyns and F. N. Davey, *The Riddle of the New Testament*, 1931; C. H. Dodd, *History and the Gospel*, 1938; D. M. Baillie, *God Was in Christ*, 1948, esp. Ch. II: 'Why the Jesus of History?'—Among current essays on the problem: F. C. Grant, 'The Spiritual Christ', *JBL* LIV, 1935, 1–15; Donald W. Riddle, 'Jesus in Modern Research', *The Journal of Religion* XVII, 1937, 170–82; T. W. Manson, 'The Life of Jesus: A Study of the Available Materials', *Bulletin of the John Rylands Library* XXVII, 1942–3, 323–37, and 'The Life of Jesus: Some Tendencies in Present-day Research', *The Background of the New Testament and its Eschatology*, ed. W. D. Davies and D. Daube, 1956, 211–21; Donald T. Rowlingson, 'On the Neglect of the Jesus of History', *Religion in Life* XX, 1950–51, 541–52; Allan Barr, 'Bultmann's Estimate of Jesus', *Scottish Journal of Theology* VII, 1954, 337–52; Raymond T. Stamm, 'New Testament Literature, 1954: II. Jesus and the Gospels he Inspired', *Interpretation* IX, 1955, 339–59; E. E. Tilden, 'New Testament Literature, 1955 and 1956 (to Midsummer)', *Interpretation* XI, 1957, 71–85 esp. 74–75.—A symposium on the question 'Is it Possible to Write a Life

quite different kind of quest based upon new premises, procedures and objectives, a quest which may well succeed in a way the other did not. For a new and promising point of departure has been worked out by precisely those scholars who are most acutely aware of the difficulties of the previous quest.[1] As a matter of fact this new development is recognized in its full significance only when one observes that it forms a central thrust in a second, 'post-Bultmannian' phase of post-war German theology.

Clearly the first phase of post-war German theology was the rise of the Bultmannian position to the centre of debate. The cumulative weight of Bultmann's prodigious career, focused into the concrete programme of demythologizing, burst like a meteor into the void caused by the attrition of the Nazi ideology, the war and post-war collapse, and the passing of such leading New Testament scholars as Lietzmann, Büchsel, Behm, von Soden, Loh-

---

of Christ' (*ExpT* LII, 1941–2, 60–65, 175–7, 248–51), with contributions by Vincent Taylor, C. J. Cadoux and T. W. Manson, is noteworthy for the unanimous rejection of the possibility of a real 'biography', and the almost equally unanimous assumption of a mediating position which is merely a sobered version of the original quest. Each contributor has subsequently published his life of Christ: Vincent Taylor, *The Life and Ministry of Jesus*, 1955; C. J. Cadoux, *Life of Jesus*, 1948; T. W. Manson, *The Servant-Messiah: A Study of the Public Ministry of Jesus*, 1953. A cross-section of views is found in Thomas S. Kepler, *Contemporary Thinking about Jesus; An Anthology*, 1944, and H. D. A. Major, T. W. Manson, C. J. Wright, *The Mission and Message of Jesus; An Exposition of the Gospels in the Light of Modern Research*, 1937. The most important American biography is probably still S. J. Case, *Jesus—A New Biography*, 1927. The difficulty of the quest found its classic English expression in R. H. Lightfoot's *History and Interpretation in the Gospels* (The Bampton Lectures for 1934). Steps in the direction of a new approach are found in R. C. Johnson, 'The Jesus of History and the Christian Faith', *Theology Today*, X, 1953, 170–84; W. Norman Pittenger, 'The Problem of the Historical Jesus', *Anglican Theological Review*, XXXVI, 1954, 89–93; R. H. Fuller, *The Mission and Achievement of Jesus*, 1954, and 'Some Problems of New Testament Christology', *Anglican Theological Review*, XXXVIII, 1956, 146–52; and the books of John Knox: *The Man Christ Jesus*, 1942; *Christ the Lord*, 1945; *On the Meaning of Christ*, 1947 (these now in one vol., *Jesus: Lord and Christ*, 1958); *The Death of Christ*, 1958. Cf. also my article, 'The Historical Jesus and the Church's Kerygma', *Religion in Life*, XXVI, 1956–7, 40–49.

[1] It is significant that these scholars feel most free to move toward a new quest when the context makes it clear that they accept the basic discoveries leading to the rejection of the nineteenth-century quest. Consequently they make a point of remaining critical toward treatments of Jesus which continue the original quest by neglecting the factors which brought it largely to

meyer, Kittel, Dibelius, and Schniewind. Such pupils of Bultmann as Ernst Käsemann (Tübingen), Günther Bornkamm (Heidelberg), Ernst Fuchs (Marburg), Erich Dinkler (Bonn), and Hans Conzelmann (Göttingen) have proven sufficiently distinguished to rise into the leading professorial positions, and a theological affinity to Gogarten and Tillich has provided a broad theological context. Bultmann himself provided a pre-established *rapprochement* with the dominant cultural trend in Germany centring in the existentialism of Martin Heidegger. His own monumental *Theology of the New Testament* provided the theological synthesis of the day, as did Barth's *Romans* a generation ago, and Harnack's *What is Christianity?* at the turn of the century. Consequently Germany is just as nearly 'Bultmannian' today as it was 'Barthian' a generation ago, 'Ritschlian' half a century or more ago, and 'Hegelian' still earlier; and Bultmann's works and ideas have

---

an end. This critical attitude is apparent, e.g. in Ernst Käsemann's reviews of the German editions of Lagrange's *L'Evangile de Jésus-Christ* (*VuF; Theol. Jahresbericht* for 1947–8 [1950], 218) and William Manson's *Jesus the Messiah* (*VuF; Theol. Jahresbericht* for 1953–5 [1956], 165–7). Cf. similarly Günther Bornkamm's review of Lagrange (*TLZ* LXXXII, 1957, 270 f.), and Hermann Diem's comments on Manson's work in his *Theologie II*, 1955, 77 f., 119 f. On the other hand Käsemann's review of the new edition of Bultmann's *Jesus* (*VuF; Theol. Jahresbericht* for 1949–50 [1952], 197) makes an initial effort to transcend the Bultmannian position in the direction of a new quest. Similarly a lecture to non-theologians ('Zum Thema der Nichtobjektivierbarkeit', *EvTh* XII, 1952–3, 455–66, esp. 463–6) reiterates the dominant contemporary German position opposing the conventional type of quest, while a lecture before 'old Marburgers' (i.e. Bultmannians) seeks to move beyond that consensus (cf. p. 12, n. 1 below). The turning-point of this lecture (133 f.), in re-evaluating the nineteenth-century quest and introducing the idea of a two-front war against docetism as well as historicism, echoes a lecture of 1933 by a leading form critic, Karl Ludwig Schmidt ('Das Christuszeugnis der synoptischen Evangelien', in *Jesus Christus im Zeugnis der Heiligen Schrift und der Kirche*, Beiheft 2 of *EvTh*, 2nd ed. 1936, 7–33). Similarly Käsemann's most recent attempt to move toward the historical Jesus ('Neutestamentliche Fragen von heute', *ZTK* LIV, 1957, 1–21, esp. 11 f.) is made in spite of the danger of a return to the nineteenth century seen in Stauffer's *Jesus: Gestalt und Geschichte* (and in the work of Joachim Jeremias), and is instigated by Günther Bornkamm's *Jesus of Nazareth* (and by the work of another Bultmannian Ernst Fuchs), and falls within the context of the first thoroughgoing criticism of Bultmann's *Theology of the New Testament* to come from within the Bultmannian group. Thus we observe a consistent effort to distinguish clearly any new quest from the original quest which still continues outside Germany.

become Germany's dominant theological export throughout the world.

One might well expect that the result of this first post-war phase would be a period of Bultmannian scholasticism. Instead we seem to be entering a new phase characterized by a critical restudy of the Bultmannian position by his leading pupils—itself a rare tribute to the spirit of free and critical scholarship represented by Bultmann. This second phase of post-war German theology may be designated as 'post-Bultmannian' in the stricter sense: led by outstanding pupils of Bultmann, it is based upon a thorough appreciation of the achievements of Bultmann's brilliant career, and could not have taken place without those achievements. Yet it sees its task as that of carrying through a critical revision of Bultmann's position, out of which revision the theological synthesis of the future will grow. The first part of this new programme to get seriously under way is with regard to the problem of the historical Jesus.

B. THE 'POST-BULTMANNIAN' QUEST OF THE HISTORICAL
JESUS

The German repudiation of the quest of the historical Jesus at the opening of the century found its definitive crystallization in the scholarship of Rudolf Bultmann. His form-critical research tended to confirm the view that such a quest is impossible, and his existential theology carried through the thesis that such a quest is illegitimate. Therefore it is not surprising that the critical restudy of his position by his pupils should begin here.

The discussion was formally opened in 1953 by Ernst Käsemann, who presented an address to a meeting of 'old Marburgers' (i.e. Bultmannians) on 'The Problem of the Historical Jesus'.[1] He moved beyond a recognition of the validity of much of Bultmann's position, to argue that since something can be known about the historical Jesus, we must concern ourselves with

[1]'Das Problem des historischen Jesus', *ZTK* LI, 1954, 125–53. This view was already suggested in his address 'Probleme neutestamentlicher Arbeit in Deutschland', in *Die Freiheit des Evangeliums und die Ordnung der Gesellschaft* (*Beiträge zur EvTh* XV, 1952), 149–52. Cf. also note on p. 11 above.

working it out, if we do not wish ultimately to find ourselves committed to a mythological Lord. The crucial issue is identified in 'the question as to the continuity of the gospel in the discontinuity of the times and the variation of the *kerygma*',[1] i.e. whether the proclamation of the exalted Lord through the Church is in some kind of recognizable continuity with the preaching of the historical Jesus, and consequently whether the exalted Lord is in continuity with Jesus of Nazareth.

Käsemann's move toward reopening the quest of the historical Jesus has met with a rapid and largely favourable response from the various segments of German-language theology. Traditionally conservative theology has inherited liberalism's original position with regard to the historical Jesus.[2] It is therefore not surprising to find Käsemann's view advocated by spokesmen for Roman Catholicism,[3] Scandinavian theology,[4] and non-Bultmannian Germans.[5] And the new quest has found the support of Joachim Jeremias,[6] who perhaps more than any other is the custodian of the heritage of detailed and exacting philological, environmental research about Jesus, which is perhaps the most permanent contribution of the original quest. Furthermore, in typical German style, the current discussion has produced a doctoral dissertation,[7]

---

[1] *ZTK* LI, 1954, 152.
[2] This nonchalant reversal of position has not passed without comment, cf. Käsemann, *Beiträge zur EvTh* XV, 149; Hermann Diem, *Theologie: Dogmatik*, 1955, 76–79; Peter Biehl, *TR*, n.F. XXIV, 1957–8, 54–55; Vincent Taylor, *The Life and Ministry of Jesus*, 1945, 19–20.
[3] Franz Mussner, 'Der historische Jesus und der Christus des Glaubens', *BZ*, n.F. I, 1957, 224–52. René Marlé, *Bultmann et l'interprétation du Nouveau Testament* (*Théologie*, No. 33, 1956), Ch. V, 'Le problème de Jésus', 142–72.
[4] Nils Alstrup Dahl, 'Der historische Jesus als geschichtswissenschaftliches und theologisches Problem', *KuD* I, 1955, 104–32. Harald Riesenfeld, 'Evangelierna och den historiske Jesus', *Svensk Exegetisk Årsbok* XX, 1955, 25–57 (cf. also his opening address at the Oxford Congress on 'The Four Gospels in 1957', *The Gospel Tradition and its Beginnings; A Study in the Limits of 'Formgeschichte'*). Erik Sjöberg, *Der verborgene Menschensohn in den Evangelien*, 1955, 214–18.
[5] Otto Michel, 'Der "historische Jesus" und das theologische Gewissensproblem', *EvTh* XV, 1955, 349–63.
[6] 'Der gegenwärtige Stand der Debatte um das Problem des historischen Jesus', *Wissenschaftliche Zeitschrift der Ernst Moritz Arndt-Universität Greifswald. Gesellschafts- und sprachwissenschaftliche Reihe*, Nr. 3, VI, 1956–7, 165–70.
[7] Hans-Hinrich Jenssen, *Die Bedeutung des historischen Jesus Christus für die*

a contribution by a non-theologian,[1] a discussion of the discussion,[2] and an extremist who clearly went too far.[3] Certainly the most significant aspect of the continuing discussion is the response of leading representatives from the predominant Bultmannian and Barthian segments of German theology.

Käsemann's initial proposal of a new quest arose from the problem of the relation of Jesus' *message* to the Church's *kerygma*. This was soon followed from the Bultmannian side by a parallel proposal on the part of Ernst Fuchs,[4] who concentrated upon Jesus' *conduct* as 'the real context of his preaching'. 'What did

---

Entmythologisierung in der Predigt, a Berlin dissertation, unpublished but briefly summarized by the author, *TLZ* LXXXI, 1956, 491 f. Ch. III argues: 'The fact of the mere *existence* (*Da*sein) of a man to whom the *kerygma* appeals as "legitimation" does not free modern man, who is all too aware of the possibility of apotheosis in the history of religion, from the doubt that Christian faith too perhaps owes its existence only to human presumption. If on the other hand it could be shown that the application to Jesus of originally mythical categories of interpretation has its thoroughly justifiable point of departure in his concrete *kind* of existence (*Sosein*), then this would be a decisive pastoral aid. It is our thesis that there is this possibility of indicating such points of departure in the concrete kind of life Jesus lived, and that for pastoral reasons we must make full use of this possibility in preaching and catechetical instruction. Consequently we do not—as is so frequent today—regard demythologizing as a liberation from an appeal to the concrete kind of life Jesus Christ lived, but rather as a renewed and deepened return to it.'

[1]E. Heitsch, 'Die Aporie des historischen Jesus als Problem theologischer Hermeneutik', *ZTK* LIII, 1956, 193–210.

[2]Peter Biehl, 'Zur Frage nach dem historischen Jesus', *op. cit.*, 54–76.

[3]Ethelbert Stauffer, *Jesus: Gestalt und Geschichte*, 1957. Cf. the review by Wm. C. Robinson, Jr, in *Interpretation* XII, 1958, 82–83, and below. Not only the Bultmannians, but even such divergent viewpoints as the Barthian Hermann Diem (*Theologie* II, 77) and the Roman Catholic Rudolf Schnackenburg concur in the latter's judgement (*BZ*, n.F. I, 1957, 314): 'Scholarship will judge that Stauffer has fallen back into the error of the earlier "Lives of Jesus", and that his attempt has failed, even when he stimulates new approaches.'

[4]'Die Frage nach dem historischen Jesus', *ZTK* LIII, 1956, 210–29, esp. 219 f. 'Glaube und Geschichte im Blick auf die Frage nach dem historischen Jesus. Eine Auseinandersetzung mit G. Bornkamms Buch über "Jesus von Nazareth"', *ZTK* LIV, 1957, 117–56. 'Bemerkungen zur Gleichnisauslegung', *TLZ* LXXIX, 1954, 345–8. *Hermeneutik*, 1954, esp. 219–30 ('Gleichnis und Parabel'). *Das Programm der Entmythologisierung*, 9, and *Das urchristliche Sakramentsverständnis*, 37–41 (Hefte 3, 1954, and 8, 1958, of the *Schriftenreihe der Kirchlich-Theologischen Sozietät in Württemberg*). 'Die der Theologie durch die historisch-kritische Methode auferlegte Besinnung', *EvTh* XVIII, 1958, 256–68. 'Jesus und der Glaube', *ZTK* LV, 1958, Heft 2.

Jesus do? We said he celebrated the eschatological meal with tax-gatherers and sinners (Matt. 11.19 par.), and we designated precisely this meal as the act of goodness supplied in advance to them all by Jesus. This means: Jesus forwent the publication of his own private eschatological experiences; rather he determined only to draw the consequences from them and to begin here on earth with the work of God visible only in heaven! This is why he celebrates his meal. *It is just this that is Jesus' real deed.*' What is here said of the eschatological meals open to all is then generalized to an interpretation of Jesus' conduct as a whole: 'This conduct is neither that of a prophet nor that of a sage, but rather the conduct of a man who dares to act in God's stead, by (as must always be added) calling near to him sinners who apart from him would have to flee from God.' This conduct, maintaining that God's will is a gracious will, by implication also claims to be divine action, and it was this claim latent in Jesus' conduct which led to opposition and to his death (Mark 3.6).

When Fuchs comes to Jesus' message, he presents it as dependent upon Jesus' action. For this view Fuchs appeals to the parables, which were often spoken in the setting of the eschatological meals: 'Jesus supplied his disciples with the interpretation of his parabolic language by an act of goodness.' 'It is consequently not the case, that first the parable clarifies Jesus' conduct —although Jesus makes use of it in defence of himself; rather it is the other way around: Jesus' conduct explains the will of God with a parable which can be read out of his conduct.' Thus in Jesus' mouth the parables are 'a witness to himself', and 'apply primarily to our relation to Jesus himself'. This approach to the parables is then generalized into an approach to all Jesus' teaching: 'For if we see this aright, then it is to be expected that certainly Jesus' words . . . generally reflect his conduct historically.' 'Jesus wishes only to be understood on the basis of his decision, his deed.' This concentration in Jesus' teaching upon his action made it possible for the disciples to conceive of his death also as divine action, which in turn led to the primitive Christian sacraments as custodians of 'Jesus' understanding of himself'. Thus

Fuchs has carried through with regard to Jesus' action the same thesis which Käsemann presented with regard to his message: in the message and action of Jesus is implicit an eschatological understanding of his person, which becomes explicit in the *kerygma* of the primitive Church.

The initiative of Käsemann and Fuchs in proposing a new quest of the historical Jesus has produced its first tangible results in the appearance in 1956 of Günther Bornkamm's monograph *Jesus of Nazareth*.[1] This is the first book on the historical Jesus to issue from the Bultmannian school since Bultmann's own *Jesus and the Word* appeared thirty years earlier. However the impetus provided by the proposal of a new quest is not only evident in the very fact that Bornkamm's book appeared, but is also evident in its distinctive divergences from Bultmann's own traditional presentation. For these divergences express the newly awakened concern for the message and conduct of Jesus in their relation to the *kerygma*.

Bornkamm does not focus his presentation on Jesus' 'word', as did Bultmann, but concerns himself as well with the events of Jesus' life, as did Fuchs. In addition to chapters on Jesus' disciples (Ch. VI) and his final journey to Jerusalem (Ch. VII), Bornkamm risks an introductory chapter which collects whatever general biographical information is available about Jesus into what amounts to a personality sketch. The significance of this chapter (III) lies in its attempt to describe the human impression Jesus made upon people in a way clearly suggestive of the meaning Jesus has for faith, as if a human contact with Jesus were—at least potentially—an encounter with the *kerygma*.

Buttressed by the context of Jesus' conduct,[2] Bornkamm's presentation of Jesus' message diverges from Bultmann's typical emphasis upon the future, of which Jesus' action in the present were but a sign calling for decision. Instead, a primary emphasis

[1]Cf. my review, *JBL* LXXVI, 1957, 310–13. The English translation appeared in 1960. Page numbers here refer to the English edition, although quotations are direct translations from the German.

[2]It is significant that Fuchs' key correlation between the eschatological meals and the parables is carried through, 81.

falls upon the present: 'Unmediated presence is always the characteristic of Jesus' words, appearance and action, within a world which . . . had lost the present, since it lived . . . between past and future, between traditions and promises or threats' (58). This is not to say that Bornkamm has moved to the position of 'realized eschatology' (91); rather he sees (with Bultmann) the tension between future and present as inherent in the involvement of the imperative in the indicative, i.e. inherent in the historical understanding of the self. But it does mean that he emphasizes more clearly than has been customary for Bultmann the continuity between Jesus' message and the Church's *kerygma*.

Bultmann's classical distinction between Jesus and Paul had been: What for Jesus is future is for Paul past and present, since the shift of aeons separates them, so that Jesus preached the law and the promise, while Paul preached the gospel.[1] This has become in Bornkamm the distinction between John the Baptist and Jesus. John is the 'sentinel at the frontier between the aeons' (51); the difference between John and Jesus is that 'between eleventh and twelfth hour' (67); and 'the contemporizing of this reality of God is the real mystery of Jesus' (62). Therefore Bornkamm's discussion of the messianic problem (Ch. VIII) does not confine itself to the view (shared with Bultmann) that Jesus made no claims to messianic titles, but goes on to explain the absence of any such special topic in Jesus' teaching by the view that 'the "messianic" aspect of his being is enclosed *in* his word and act, and in the unmediatedness of his historical appearance' (178). This leads to a final chapter (IX : 'Jesus Christ') in which a continuity between the historical Jesus and the Church's *kerygma* is sketched. In the Easter experience the disciples were assured 'that God himself had intervened with almighty hand in the wicked and rebellious activity of the world, and had snatched this Jesus of Nazareth from the power of sin and death which had risen up against him, and installed him as Lord of the world.' Easter 'is thus at the same time the inbreaking of the new world of God into this old world branded by sin and death, the setting up and beginning of his

[1]*GuV* I, 200 f., 316.

reign. . . . We note how here Jesus' own message of the coming
reign of God rings out again in new form, only that he himself
with his death and resurrection has now entered into this message
and become its centre' (183 f.). Here it is clear that Jesus' eschatological message, including his eschatological interpretation of his
own conduct, has been continued in christological terms by the
Easter faith and the Christian *kerygma*.

Hans Conzelmann[1] has united these various lines of development into a unified view of Jesus' eschatology and his person, in
which christology replaces chronology as the basic meaning of
Jesus' message: the kingdom which Jesus proclaims is future, but
the 'interim' is of no positive significance to him. Rather Jesus
confronts man with an unmediated and consequently determina-
tive encounter with the kingdom. This is the common significance of various themes which when taken literally could be
contradictory: the nearness of the kingdom, the suddenness of its
coming, and Jesus himself as the last sign. None of this is meant
by Jesus temporally, but only existentially. Although the nearness
is presented temporally, its 'meaning lies in qualifying the human
situation in view of the coming of the kingdom'. Predictions of
coming reward and punishment, like the present beatitudes and
woes, represent the alternatives of salvation or lostness involved
in one's present situation. Hence Jesus' message of salvation and
his call for repentance 'form together the absolute determination
of human existence'.

Put the other way round, 'existing means nothing more than
comprehending the signs', i.e. Jesus' action. If Jesus' eschatology
seems intentionally to ignore time, this is only because it intentionally centres in his person. He 'connects the hope of salvation
with his person to the extent that he sees the kingdom effective
in his deeds and understands his preaching as the last word of
God before the end.' Thus his eschatology involves an 'indirect'
christology: 'If the kingdom is *so* near that it casts *this* shadow,
then the "observer" no longer has it before him, in the sense

[1]'Eschatologie: IV, im Urchristentum', *RGG*, 3rd ed., II, 1958, 665–72,
esp. 666–8; 'Gegenwart und Zukunft in der synoptischen Tradition', *ZTK*
LIV, 1957 (appeared Summer 1958), 277–96, esp. 286–8.

that he could still observe it from a certain distance; rather is he at that instant fully claimed. Jesus does not give a new answer to the question "When?"—in that case he would still be an apocalypticist—, but rather he supersedes this question as such.'

C. BULTMANN'S SHIFT IN POSITION

Certainly anyone who has followed this 'post-Bultmannian' development within Germany cannot fail to wonder how Bultmann himself reacts to this trend, a trend which certainly diverges from the 'classical' Bultmannian position, but which nonetheless works largely upon Bultmannian presuppositions and can in fact appeal to an undercurrent in Bultmann's writings which already moves in this direction.[1] It is therefore quite significant that a

[1] A summary of the classical Bultmannian position is found in the following quotation (*GuV* I, 208): 'So one may not go back behind the *kerygma*, using it as a "source", in order to reconstruct a "historical Jesus" with his "messianic consciousness", his "inwardness" or his "heroism". That would be precisely the Christ according to the flesh, who is gone. Not the historical Jesus, but Jesus Christ, the proclaimed, is the Lord.' However the various factors in this statement leading up to a repudiation of a quest of the historical Jesus do not, when analysed, necessitate this conclusion, except in terms of the original quest. The possibility of uniting these factors with the acceptance of a new kind of quest becomes visible from time to time in Bultmann's own writing. His *Jesus and the Word* of 1926 maintains in this regard a somewhat ambiguous role in the context of his total position. Käsemann (*ZTK* LI, 1954, 125) holds that *Jesus and the Word* intentionally avoids distinguishing between Jesus and the oldest *kerygma*, as if the relevance of *Jesus and the Word* lay for Bultmann in its inclusion of the *kerygma*; while Bultmann himself says (*Kerygma and Myth*, 1953, 117) that his book on Jesus is not *kerygma*. He can seem to express a complete lack of interest in Jesus: 'The Christ according to the flesh does not concern us; how things looked in Jesus' heart I do not know and do not wish to know' (*GuV* I, 101). However this remark of 1927 must be understood in terms of his rejection of psychologism and his disapproval of a personality cult, as in the preface to *Jesus and the Word* of 1926, where the positive alternative is given. In the case of great men, '*their* interest was not their personality, but their work', which he seeks to present in *Jesus and the Word*. In this preface he expresses a lack of interest in the question as to whether Jesus claimed for himself messianic titles. However this is because the answer to such a question would not provide a real solution to the problem of Jesus' significance, which Bultmann himself answers positively (*GuV* I, 1933, 265f.): 'Whether or not he knew himself as Messiah makes no difference. It would only indicate that he brought to consciousness the character of his action as decisive by making use of a Jewish concept of the day. But to be sure his call to decision implies a christology. . . . When the primitive Church names him the Messiah, she in her way brings to expression that she understood him.' Hence positive statements of the relation of Jesus'

recent article by Bultmann[1] seems to be by implication a defence of Käsemann's position against an initial criticism by the Barthian Hermann Diem:[2] Diem had maintained that when all is said and done Käsemann has presented Jesus as only proclaiming 'general religious and moral truths' about 'the freedom of the children of God', rather than a message in continuity with the Church's *kerygma*. For Käsemann doubts that Jesus claimed to be Son of Man and says instead: 'Jesus came . . . to say how things stand with the kingdom that has dawned, namely that God has drawn near man in grace and requirement. He brought and lived the freedom of the children of God, who remain children and free only so long as they find in the Father their Lord.'[3]

Bultmann points out that eternal truths, when used in concrete proclamation, can become historical encounter. Already in this sense he recognizes that Jesus' teachings were used by the primitive Church as kerygmatic proclamation of the exalted Lord: 'One can hardly object that Jesus' preaching was after all not Christian preaching, on the grounds that Christian preaching proclaims him, but was not proclaimed by him. Even if here we completely ignore the question, in what sense Jesus' preaching could perhaps after all be designated a hidden or secret Christian preaching, in any case his preaching was taken up into Christian preaching and became a part of the proclamation in which the Proclaimed is at the same time present as the Proclaimer' (246). However this is a purely formal use of Jesus' teachings, just as many 'general truths' can be used in concrete proclamation. Bultmann recognizes that the problem of the relation of Jesus' teaching to the Church's

message to the Church's *kerygma* do occur: *GuV* I, 205; *Theology of the New Testament* I, 1951 (Ger. ed. 1948), 42 ff. And this concern of Bultmann's for the historical Jesus has been on occasion detected, e.g. by Walther Eltester, *ZNTW* XXXIII, 1950–1, 276, and Peter Biehl, *TR*, n.F. XXIV, 1957–8, 76.

[1]'Allgemeine Wahrheit und christliche Verkündigung', *ZTK* LIV, 1957, 244–54. (This fascicle of *ZTK* actually appeared in Jan. 1958.) Bultmann had already shared in the move toward a new liberalism signalled by the reappearance of the *Zeitschrift für Theologie und Kirche* in 1950. Cf. his introduction to the semi-centennial edition of Harnack's *What is Christianity?* (1950; Eng. ed. 1957).

[2]*Theologie* II, 124.

[3]*ZTK* LI, 1954, 151.

kerygma—i.e. the by-passed question of the sense in which Jesus'
preaching is Christian—goes deeper. 'This does not yet make it
clear why the Proclaimer necessarily became the Proclaimed, unless it could be shown that Jesus' preaching of the law was
differentiated from every other preaching of the law by being at
the same time the proclamation of God's grace, which not only
assumes freedom, but also grants it' (253).

At this point those accustomed to Bultmann's earlier distinction
of Jesus from Paul in terms of law and gospel,[1] and his subsequent classification of Jesus within Judaism[2] as only a presupposition of New Testament theology,[3] would expect him
simply to repeat that position. But instead, he lays hold of Fuchs'
concept of Jesus' conduct as God's goodness in action, and comes
to the conclusion that Jesus' message is after all grace, i.e. 'after
all a hidden or secret Christian preaching': 'Such calls for decision
as Matt. 11.6; Luke 12.8 f., are, by calling for decision with regard
to his person, at the same time words of promise, of grace: it is
at this very moment that the gift of freedom is offered to the
hearer. If the one who calls for decision is the "glutton and
drunkard, the friend of tax collectors and sinners" (Luke 7.34 f.;
Matt. 11.19), does this not mean that he who proclaims the radical
requirement of God at the same time speaks the word of grace?
If the tax collectors and harlots enter the kingdom of God before
the officially "righteous" (Matt. 21.31), then it is because those
who understand God's requirement are those who have received
grace. And when the condition runs: "Whoever does not receive
the kingdom of God like a child shall not enter it" (Mark 10.15),
then certainly the condition contains at the same time the assurance of grace' (254). Bultmann himself seems to have adjusted
to the 'post-Bultmannian' move of his pupils[4] at least with
regard to grace in the historical Jesus and the *kerygma*.

[1]*GuV* I, 1933, 200 f.
[2]*Primitive Christianity in its Contemporary Setting,* 1956 (Ger. ed. 1949).
[3]*Theology of the New Testament* I, 3.
[4]This does not alter the fact that Bultmann's pupils conceive of the new
quest as 'post-Bultmannian' rather than simply 'Bultmannian'; cf. the critical
context in which it is presented by Käsemann, esp. 'Neutestamentliche
Fragen von heute', *ZTK* LIV, 1957, 1–21.

When we apply this position to Diem's original criticism of Käsemann, that the latter presented Jesus as only teaching general truths rather than the *kerygma*, it becomes clear that Diem has overlooked the crucial point: Käsemann went beyond the view that Jesus *taught* God's fatherhood and man's freedom, to the assertion that 'God has *drawn near* man in grace and requirement,' and Jesus '*brought* and *lived* the freedom of the children of God'. Between the false alternatives of 'just general truths' or 'explicit claims to messianic titles' there lies in Jesus' public ministry a whole area of eschatological action accompanied by theological commentary which Diem overlooked, and wherein resides both the historical and the theological point of departure for the Church's *kerygma*, and thus the crucial area of research for a new quest of the historical Jesus.

D. THE BARTHIAN RAPPROCHEMENT

The movement we have sketched within the historical research of New Testament scholars largely under Bultmannian influence is to a certain extent parallel to the increasingly positive evaluation of history on the part of Karl Barth,[1] and a reawakening concern for the historical Jesus on the part of systematic theologians closely associated with him.[2] Perhaps the most significant instance of this trend is the shift of Hermann Diem from his initial attitude of considerable reserve to an acceptance of the basic position of Käsemann. Diem's basic position[3] is that the New Testament

[1] Cf. specifically the basic christological sections of his volumes on reconciliation (*Church Dogmatics* IV. 1, 2).

[2] E.g. Fritz Lieb, 'Die Geschichte Jesu Christi in Kerygma und Historie. Ein Beitrag zum Gespräch mit Rudolf Bultmann', in *Antwort* (Barth Festschrift, 1956), 582–95. Further '"Geschichte und Heilsgeschichte in der Theologie Rudolf Bultmanns"' (on Heinrich Ott's book of that title), *EvTh* XV, 1955, 507–22.

[3] *Theologie als kirchliche Wissenschaft. Handreichung zur Einübung ihrer Probleme,* 1951 (cited as *Theologie* I), esp. Para. 5: 'Die Aufgaben und Probleme für den Historiker', and Para. 6: 'Der Historiker als kirchlicher Theologe', 57–69; and Band II: *Dogmatik. Ihr Weg zwischen Historismus und Existentialismus,* 1955 (cited as *Theologie* II), esp. Para. 3: 'Die Bedeutung des historischen Jesus für Verkündigung, Lehre und Glauben der Kirche', and Para. 4: 'Die Geschichte von Jesus Christus, der sich selbst verkündigt', 76–131. Para. 4 has also been published separately (1955). With Diem's basic position cf. also Peter Biehl, *TR*, n.F. XXIV, 1957–8, 58–61.

proclaims a Jesus Christ who proclaims himself. 'This history of
the proclamation is the object of historical research in the New
Testament which we seek, and which is the only legitimate object
of such historical research according to the New Testament's
understanding of itself.'[1] But rather than implying by this, according to his original Barthian position,[2] that one cannot enquire behind the evangelist's message to that of Jesus,[3] Diem
now recognizes that 'we must search back to that first phase of
the history of the proclamation, the proclamation of the earthly
Jesus himself'.[4] For this historical question of the continuity of
the proclamation from Jesus to the Church is recognized as the
theological question as to whether the Church's Lord is a myth.
For Diem concedes that a negative answer to the historical question would 'negatively prejudice' the theological question as to
the truth of the gospel. Consequently he concerns himself with
the historical question sufficiently seriously to trace,[5] in one
instance, the term 'Son of Man' in the Gospels, the continuity

[1] *Der irdische Jesus und der Christus des Glaubens* (*SgV* 215, 1957), 9.

[2] Diem (*Theologie* II, 129) quotes Barth (*Church Dogmatics,* I. 2, 494): '. . . the
exegesis of canonical Scripture as such, the coherent exposition of Genesis,
Isaiah, the Gospel of Matthew, etc. according to their present status and com-
pass, is again recognized and undertaken as in the last resort the *only* possible
goal of biblical scholarship. . . . The *historical truth* which in its own way
biblical scholarship does have to mediate is the true *meaning and context of the
biblical texts as such.*' (Barth's italics.) Consequently Diem permits recourse
behind the text only to the extent needed to establish the 'meaning and context of the biblical texts as such', i.e. one can concern oneself with the
history of the origin of the present text only in order to establish how the
individual witnesses arrived at their present canonical form and are to be
understood (*Theologie* II, 130 f.).

[3] *Theologie* II, 117, 127, 129: 'From the very beginning we have declared
ourselves not interested in this historical reconstruction of Jesus' proclamation.' 'The history of Jesus Christ encounters us only in the history of the
proclamation of this history, and can be laid hold of historically only in the
latter. Consequently (the historian's) subject-matter can only be the history
of the proclamation present in the texts.' 'Consequently the task of this research would now no longer be to enquire of the text concerning a history
which lies behind it and on which it would report, but rather to enquire of
the history of the statements of the text itself. In the formation of the text
the history of the proclamation becomes visible, for the history of the text is
itself the only historically attainable segment of this history of the proclamation.'

[4] *Der irdische Jesus und der Christus des Glaubens,* 12.

[5] *Ibid.,* 15 f.

between Jesus' message and the Church's witness: although Jesus may never have called himself Son of Man, he did say that acquittal by the Son of Man in the eschatological judgement was dependent upon one's present relation to himself (Mark 8.38 par.). Thus the content of salvation is dependent on Jesus, and it was this which the Church explicated by attributing to him the title of bringer of salvation (i.e. the title Son of Man). Here Diem has clearly moved to the position of the advocates of the new quest, both by accepting—in terms almost identical with those of Käsemann—the theological validity of the new quest, and by adopting the basic method of the new quest, which consists in moving below the surface of terms and even concepts to the level of theological meaning and existential significance.[1]

From this survey of current German discussion we may conclude that the proposal of a new quest of the historical Jesus, originally made within the context of the 'post-Bultmannian' direction of leading pupils of Bultmann, has broadened itself, not only in traditionally conservative circles, but also by support from the Barthian side as well as from Bultmann himself.[2] A concen-

[1] A somewhat analogous direction is also indicated by Jeremias, 'Der gegenwärtige Stand der Debatte um das Problem des historischen Jesus', 169 f.: 'Everywhere in Jesus' proclamation we strike upon this ultimate claim, i.e. we strike upon the same claim for faith which the *kerygma* directs to us. Here something which is quite simple and obvious must be stated, since it is no longer obvious. Every sentence in the sources attests it to us, every verse in our Gospels hammers it in. Something has happened, something unique, something which never before existed. . . . There is no parallel for the authority which dares to address God with Abba. If we merely acknowledge the fact that the word "Abba" is Jesus' *ipsissima vox*— and I would not know how it could be contested—then, if this word is understood aright and not rendered harmless, we stand before Jesus' transcendent claim. . . . Thus example could be added to example, and the result is the same every time: when we use the critical means at our disposal with discipline and conscientiousness, we strike again and again, in our efforts concerning the historical Jesus, upon the ultimate: we are placed before God himself. . . . It is not as if [the act of] faith were taken from us or even facilitated, when exegesis shows us how his transcendent claim stands behind his every word and each of his deeds. . . . But it is true that the question of faith is inescapably posed at every turn by Jesus' words and deeds.'

[2] This *rapprochement* between German New Testament scholars largely operating upon Bultmannian presuppositions and German systematic theologians largely operating upon Barthian presuppositions is a result of the concern on both sides over the unhealthy separation of New Testament

tration of force seems to be in the making, which may well provide enough impetus to move beyond a mere proposal to a distinctive trait of theology during the coming generation.[1]

It is in this relatively propitious setting that the present work is presented, as a contribution to the new quest both by a clarification of its nature, and by an initial participation in the work of the new quest at a few significant points.

In order to enter into this discussion in such a way as to be able to make a fruitful contribution to it, it will be necessary (Ch. II) to recognize the degree of validity inherent in the arguments which brought the original quest to an end by pointing to its impossibility and illegitimacy. For only within the valid limits thus imposed can one seek in a relevant way (Ch. III) to define the sense in which a new quest may be possible, and to investigate (Ch. IV) the legitimacy of such a quest, i.e. the degree to which it is theologically permissible and necessary. Only then can one attempt (Ch. V) to get the actual work under way by laying hold of the central problem in terms of which the detailed research upon individual problems will gain its relevance.

---

research and systematic theology characteristic of Germany since the war. Cf. Käsemann, 'Probleme neutestamentlicher Arbeit in Deutschland', 138; Diem, *Theologie* II, 38 f. and *passim; Der irdische Jesus und der Christus des Glaubens*, 19. For a contribution to the discussion by a systematic theologian with Bultmannian presuppositions, cf. Gerhard Ebeling, ZTK LV, 1958, 64–109.

[1]Cf. e.g. Jeremias, 'Der gegenwärtige Stand der Debatte um das Problem des historischen Jesus', 168: 'As a matter of fact, then, the most recent theological development is moving beyond Bultmann at this very point. One sees that the question of the historical Jesus must be taken seriously, and thus the situation in contemporary New Testament research is after all not as disunited as it might seem at the first glance.'

II

THE IMPOSSIBILITY AND ILLEGITIMACY OF THE ORIGINAL QUEST

A. THE AMBIGUOUS TERM 'HISTORICAL JESUS'

'The quest of the historical Jesus' is an expression which has become familiar to us as the English title of Albert Schweitzer's book *Von Reimarus zu Wrede*. It is a poetic rendering of the German subtitle, which read literally: 'A History of Research upon the Life of Jesus'. Thus those who have read Schweitzer's book have come to sense that the expression 'historical Jesus' is closely related to modern historical research. Yet the extent to which the meaning of the term is inextricably related to historical research must be explained in some detail, if the concept is to be freed from the ambiguity which continues to haunt it.

The term 'historical Jesus' is not simply identical with 'Jesus' or 'Jesus of Nazareth', as if the adjective 'historical' were a meaningless addition. Rather the adjective is used in a technical sense, and makes a specific contribution to the total meaning of the expression. 'Historical' is used in the sense of 'things in the past which have been established by objective scholarship'.[1] Consequently the expression 'historical Jesus' comes to mean: 'What can be known of Jesus of Nazareth by means of the scientific methods of the historian.' Thus we have to do with a technical

[1] Cf. the definition of the noun 'history' from which this use of the adjective is derived, e.g. Diem, *Der irdische Jesus . . .*, 9: 'Under *Historie* we understand not the history itself which happened, but rather the ἱστορεῖν (investigation) of it, in the . . . sense of *learning about it, experiencing it, reporting about what is experienced.*' Similarly Barth defines *Historie*: 'the history which is available to man by being perceptible to him and comprehensible by him' (*KD* III.1, 84); 'ascertainable by the means and methods and especially, under the tacit presuppositions, of modern historical scholarship' (*KD* III.2, 535).

The Impossibility and Illegitimacy of the Original Quest

expression which must be recognized as such, and not automatically identified with the simple term 'Jesus'.

This technical meaning of the expression 'historical Jesus' may seem to us an unwarranted narrowing of the term 'history'. Yet such usage is nearest to the original, etymological meaning of the term 'history' (lit. 'research'). Such usage is somewhat similar to the scientist's use of the term 'nature' to refer to what in the world around us is subsumed under law by scientific research.[1] Now 'history' and 'nature' in this sense would envisage all of reality, if one assumed that objective historical scholarship and scientific research could, in theory at least, reach the whole of reality. In that case the technical usage of 'history' and 'nature' could be as comprehensive as the layman's normal meaning of 'history' as 'all that happened' and 'nature' as 'the whole world around us'.

This was in fact the assumption of the nineteenth-century quest of the historical Jesus. For this quest was initiated by the enlightenment in its effort to escape the limitations of dogma,[2] and thereby to gain access to the whole reality of the past. The quest

[1] The potentiality of this meaning inheres in the origin of the term as the Latin translation of the technical Greek term φύσις, whose etymological origin lay in the concept of growth. Thus 'nature' is the product of the growing process, which itself is grasped as conforming to law. This aspect is still echoed in the current definition (Funk and Wagnalls' New 'Standard' Dictionary of the English Language, 1952): 'A collective abstract term for the entire universe, and embracing all its existences, forces, and laws, regarded as constituting a system or unity which may be covered, however vaguely, by one conception and designated by a single term. In this meaning, however, we are obliged to recognize an attempt to blend two aspects or ways of regarding the universe which are more or less distinctly different, while both are necessary. These are: (1) The system of things and persons regarded as actually existent in space and time. . . . (2) The moulding or creative forces; the powers which account for the origins and changes of things, and for the production and evolution of the world, in accordance with some observable or purely conjectural plan or controlling ideas.' This last emphasis was brought to the centre of attention by Kant, who emphasized the epistemological aspect: 'We ourselves bring the order and conformity to law . . . into the phenomena which we call nature.' In this tradition K. Lasswitz (*Geschichte der Atomistik,* 1890, I, 80) defines nature as 'that which is objectified as temporal-spatial phenomenon by systematic thought, i.e. that which is conceptually established and thus guaranteed by law.' Cf. *Eislers Handwörterbuch der Philosophie* (2nd ed. 1922), s.v.

[2] This oft-forgotten origin of the quest has recently been emphasized by Jeremias, 'Der gegenwärtige Stand der Debatte um das Problem des historischen Jesus', 165 f.

27

of the historical Jesus was originally the quest after 'the Jesus of Nazareth who actually lived in first-century Palestine', unrestricted by the doctrinal presentations of him in Bible, creed and Church. One then proceeded to implement this alternative between orthodox christology and the Jesus of the enlightenment by appeal to the current alternatives in method. If the orthodox Christ was reached through faith and doctrine, it was readily assumed that 'the real Jesus of Nazareth' could be found by means of the newly-discovered historiography promising to narrate the past 'as it actually was'. Hence for the nineteenth century the two meanings of 'the historical Jesus' tended to coincide: 'Jesus of Nazareth as he actually was' coincided with 'the reconstruction of his biography by means of objective historical method'.

For the twentieth century this is no longer obvious. The reason for this change does not lie in any restriction of the historical-critical method in dealing with the objective data, as if there were one group of historical facts accessible to historiography,while other historical facts were in principle beyond the historian's reach.[1] Rather we have come to recognize that the objective factual level upon which the nineteenth century operated is only one dimension of history, and that a whole new dimension in the facts, a deeper and more central plane of meaning, had been largely bypassed. The nineteenth century saw the reality of the 'historical facts' as consisting largely in names, places, dates, occurrences, sequences, causes, effects—things which fall far short of being the actuality of history, if one understands by history the distinctively human, creative, unique, purposeful, which distinguishes man from nature. The dimension in which man actually exists, his 'world', the stance or outlook from which he acts, his understanding of his existence behind what he does, the way

---

[1]Such is, in fact, the view of Karl Barth (*KD* III.1, 84–88), but his view is here not characteristic of contemporary historiography. Cf. e.g. Bultmann's rejection of its use by Barth, in *Essays Philosophical and Theological*, 260 f.; Biehl's rejection of its use by Heinrich Ott (*Geschichte und Heilsgeschichte in der Theologie Rudolf Bultmanns*, 1955, 16), in his essay 'Welchen Sinn hat es, von "theologischer Ontologie" zu reden?', *ZTK*, LIII, 1956, 370; and Biehl's rejection of its use by Diem (*Theologie* II, 88), in his essay 'Zur Frage nach dem historischen Jesus', *TR*, n.F. XXIV, 1957–8, 59.

he meets his basic problems and the answer his life implies to the human dilemma, the significance he had as the environment of those who knew him, the continuing history his life produces, the possibility of existence which his life presents to me as an alternative—such matters as these have become central in an attempt to understand history. It is this deeper level of the reality of 'Jesus of Nazareth as he actually was' which was not reached by 'the reconstruction of his biography by means of objective historical method'. Consequently the two meanings of the term 'historical Jesus' no longer coincide.

Once it had become clear that nineteenth-century historical method had failed to penetrate the depths at which the reality of history lies, and consequently that its 'historical Jesus' failed to exhaust the reality of Jesus of Nazareth, it was inevitable that a re-study of historical method should follow, in an attempt to gain access to that deeper level of historical reality. But until such a method could be worked out and applied, and its results brought in, the only scientific historical reconstruction which was actually available remained that of the nineteenth century. For the time being at least, the only 'historical Jesus' available was the nineteenth-century reconstruction, now seen to fall far short of Jesus of Nazareth as he actually was. Consequently the twentieth century worked out its initial attitude toward the 'historical Jesus' in terms of the only available reconstruction, that of the nineteenth century with all its deficiencies.

This produced in the first place a recognition of the relativity of historical research even in the modern, post-enlightenment period. To say that medieval historians were subjective would not imply that historiography is inevitably subjective. But to say that the classical age of objective historical-critical research was itself historically conditioned and to this extent subjective, was to imply that historiography is inevitably limited as to the degree of objectivity and finality it can attain. Thus Lessing's old problem as to how 'accidental historical truths can serve as proofs for eternal rational truths' was deepened by the awareness that even our reconstruction of the 'historical truths' is 'accidental', i.e.

historically relative. All this was only augmented by the growing awareness in psychology, cultural anthropology, and existentialism of the basic historicity of the self, so that one no longer assumed that the historical and relative could be readily removed as merely a surface defect on an essentially natural or changelessly rational selfhood. The problem of the historian's own historicity has become a fundamental problem. Quite apart from the assumptions of Christian faith, it is easy to see that all that Jesus actually was is not likely to be fully grasped, objectively demonstrated, and definitively stated by historical research in any given period.[1] Now when we add to this the assumption that the historian's

[1] This conclusion about Jesus is in accord with the whole trend of historical research in our century. The view of F. M. Powicke, a central figure in British historiography during the first half of this century, is typical. In his address 'After Fifty Years' to the Historical Association in 1944 (*History*, XXIX, 1944, 2–16, reprinted in *Modern Historians and the Study of History*, 1955, 225–39), he said (229 f.): 'At the same time, as we look back over the last fifty years, all of us must be conscious of the *malaise* or discomfort which oppresses the thoughtful study of history. The historical student, especially if he is also a teacher of history, has never been so conscious of the significance of his subject. He is convinced, and rightly, of its importance and is beset by a public eager to know what it is all about; yet he can give no clear answers. This, at any rate, is the impression, probably the strongest impression, left upon my own mind, as I reflect upon the movement of the last half-century, and a most uncomfortable impression it is. The main reason for it is the susceptibility of all of us, whether we are historical students or not, to the sense of inadequacy to which I have already referred. The old smooth generalizations do not seem to fit, and the effort to make new ones is so faltering. . . . We are expected, willingly or unwillingly, to speak with assurance about the most mysterious and most intimate problem than can engage the mind of man, the experience of man as a social being throughout the centuries.' Similarly in his *History, Freedom and Religion*, 1938, 15 f.: 'Just as nine-tenths of our personal experience consists of instinctive or habitual acts, which we do not record even in our own memories, so it is in the past experience of peoples, nations, states. Even of what is left, the tenth part, some is consciously remembered, only to be forgotten as it is displaced by new experience, and some is too intimate to be shared with others; and so it is with peoples, nations, and states. . . . Just because history is so full of intelligence and of human purpose which eludes us, and is in its nature an incessant denial of fatalism, it can give us that sense of remoteness which we associate with fatalism. Sometimes, in the watches of the night, I have seen the whole of human experience, since mankind, as a thinking animal, loosened the hold of matter upon him—human experience with its incessant, ant-like activity, its hopes and fears, its aspirations and its despair—as a great glacier moving imperceptibly, remorselessly, and myself as a tiny flake of frozen snow upon its lowest edge, explaining the nature and the laws of the vast mass, whence it came and whither it goes.'

subject matter is God, the impossibility of the situation is more than obvious. Thus the whole Ritschlian attempt to prove Christianity historically suddenly became absurd.[1] Consequently it seems incredibly naïve when today an advocate of positivistic historicism wishes to revive the attempt to prove historically the 'absoluteness of Jesus'.[2]

Since the twentieth century worked out its initial attitude toward the 'historical Jesus' in terms of the only available reconstruction, that of the nineteenth century with all its glaring limitations, it is not surprising to find as a second consequence a tendency to disassociate the expression 'the historical Jesus' from 'Jesus of Nazareth as he actually was', and to reserve the expression for: 'What can be known of Jesus of Nazareth by means of the scientific methods of the historian'.[3] 'The historical Jesus' comes really to mean no more than 'the historian's Jesus'. The clear implication is that 'Jesus of Nazareth as he actually was' may be considerably more than or quite different from 'the historical Jesus'.

It is in this sense that one must correctly understand statements which might seem shocking if used in the other sense of the term: 'We can know very little about the historical Jesus'. If by this one means that we can know very little about Jesus of Nazareth by means of the scientific methods of the historian, so that a modern biography of him is hardly possible, such a viewpoint need not trouble the believer, although it could be a topic of

---

Cf. also Benedetto Croce, *History as the Story of Liberty*, 1941, and R. G. Collingwood, *The Idea of History*, 1946.

[1] The classical document of this sudden reversal is Martin Kähler's *Der sogenannte historische Jesus und der geschichtliche, biblische Christus* (1892). This lecture has received more serious attention during the last generation than it did when it first appeared; the second edition of 1896 was reissued in 1928, and the original edition reappeared in 1953.

[2] E. Stauffer, 'Entmythologisierung oder Realtheologie?', *KuM* II, 27.

[3] Biehl, *TR*, n.F. XXIV, 1957-8, 55, gives a typical definition of 'der historische Jesus': 'Jesus, in so far as he can be made an object of historical-critical research'. It is clear that Bultmann is making use of this definition when e.g. he says (*Kerygma and Myth*, 117): 'The Jesus of history (Ger.: der historische Jesus) is not kerygma, any more than my book was. For in the kerygma Jesus encounters us as the Christ—that is, as the eschatological phenomenon *par excellence*.'

legitimate discussion among historians. For the believer's know-ledge of Jesus has been hardly more dependent upon the his-torian's research than has his knowledge of God. Such research was as a matter of fact largely non-existent during the centuries of most fervent Christian faith. The same situation prevails with regard to another current statement: 'Christian faith is not inter-ested in the historical Jesus.' This statement is to a considerable extent true, if one understands it correctly to mean that Christians throughout the ages have been largely ignorant of and not inter-ested in 'what can be known of Jesus of Nazareth by means of the scientific methods of the historian'. The statement would become largely untrue only if one assumed it to be maintaining that Christian faith is not interested in Jesus of Nazareth.

B. THE END OF THE ORIGINAL QUEST

This discussion of the shifting meaning of the term 'historical Jesus' has already drawn attention to the basic shift in modern man's relation to history, as one of the broad and pervasive reasons why the quest came to an end. But there were also factors at work within the specific area of the study of Jesus which crystallized into the consensus that the quest is both impossible and illegitimate. It is to these factors within the discipline itself that we now wish to turn.

It is often said that Albert Schweitzer's *Quest of the Historical Jesus* marks the end of the quest. This is to a considerable extent true, if one does not take it to mean that his book *caused* the end of the quest. Undoubtedly his book was sufficiently shocking to give pause for thought. But neither of the main points he makes was such as to lead to more than a temporary suspension of the quest: 'The so-called historical Jesus of the nineteenth century biographies is really a modernization, in which Jesus is painted in the colours of modern bourgeois respectability and neo-Kantian moralism.'[1] However Schweitzer did not radicalize this insight

[1]An interesting confirmation of this philosophical origin of the prejudice Schweitzer detected in the original quest may be found in the comparison of the method of exegesis Kant proposed in 1798, and a methodological state-ment by one of the last representatives of nineteenth-century liberalism in

into a questioning of the objectivity of historical research as such, but himself presented a reconstruction of Jesus which he regarded as objective, simply because it lacked the Victorianism of

---

Germany, Hans Windisch. In *Der Streit der Fakultäten*, Kant proposed a higher form of exegesis, to supersede that current in his day. He summarized his argument as follows (108–11): 'What may be required of the *art* of biblical *interpretation* (hermeneutica sacra), since it may not be left to the laity (for it concerns a scientific system), is, in view of that which in religion is statutory: that the interpreter make clear to himself whether his statement should be understood as *authentic* or *doctrinal*.—In the first case the interpretation must be literally (philologically) appropriate to the meaning of the author; in the second case however the writer has the freedom to write into the text (philosophically) that meaning which it has in exegesis, from a moral, practical point of view (for the edification of the pupil); for faith in a mere historical sentence is dead in the sentence itself.—Although the first method may be important enough for the biblical scholar and indirectly also for the people from some practical point of view, yet the real objective of religious doctrine, to produce morally better men, can not only be missed thereby, but even hindered. . . . Therefore only the *doctrinal* interpretation, which does not need to know (empirically) what kind of meaning the holy author may have connected with his words, but rather what kind of doctrine the reason (*a priori*), in the interest of morals, can at the instigation of a saying read into the text of the Bible, only such a doctrinal interpretation is the sole evangelical, biblical method of teaching the people in true, inner and universal religion. . . . With regard to the religion of a people which has learned to reverence a holy Scripture, the doctrinal interpretation of it, which is related to the people's moral interest—edification, moral improvement, and thus blessedness—is at the same time the authentic interpretation: i.e. it is in this way that God wishes to have his will, revealed in the Bible, to be understood.' With this one can compare Hans Windisch's description of his own exegetical method (in his discussion with H. Jordan: 'Ein Briefwechsel über die Jesusfrage der Gegenwart', *ChrW* XXV, 1911, 988, quoted by Erik Beijer, 'Hans Windisch und seine Bedeutung für die neutestamentliche Wissenschaft', *ZNTW* XLVIII, 1957, 46 f.): 'The typical Jesus of modern criticism, according to the training I went through, is a man who shared many errors of his time, even with regard to religious questions; who was deeply saturated in eschatological ideas (his preaching of repentance and salvation are very intimately bound up with his expectation of the near end of the world); who however is able to lay hold also of modern hearts because of the strength of his divine seizure and because of the clarity and sharpness of his teaching. . . . I claim for myself the privilege, as do Bousset and Weinel, of modernizing the assumedly historical Jesus for practical use, i.e. to work out a figure which is similar to the Jesus of Herrmann's theology. I am fully aware that I am reading subjective interpretations into what is historically provable, and filling out gaps of scholarly research according to practical needs. Only in this procedure I have no inclination to draw near to the ecclesiastical dogma of Christ; rather I accentuate my difference.' These two quotations from Kant and Windisch are related to each other as prophecy and fulfilment, and tend to document this aspect of Schweitzer's thesis.

the classical lives of Christ. Nor did his insight lead him to doubt the appropriateness of the sources for the kind of chronological biography he and his predecessors tried to write. Instead he rejected the doubts of Wrede at this point, and to this extent is himself one of the last spokesmen for the nineteenth-century view of the sources. From his point of view the rejection of the nineteenth-century biographies as modernizations need in no sense involve a rejection of the quest itself, for the simple reason that an initial prejudice once detected does not justify the permanent end of a scholarly project.

The other main point of Schweitzer's presentation is that the real Jesus of Nazareth was actually less modern than the Nicene Christ one had originally intended to replace. Schweitzer put it bluntly: Jesus was the high water mark of Jewish apocalypticism. Thus the theological value of the original quest in proving the Ritschlian system was reversed. Schweitzer had little personal sympathy for eschatology, and saw in it no potentiality for theology today. Consequently his construction was characterized by a crudity and misunderstanding inevitable in any appraisal of history from an inner distance. He remained a Ritschlian in his heart, and never dreamed that he would live to see Jesus' eschatology become the core of modern theology. For theology has outlived the initial shock, and, in the movement stemming from Karl Barth, has learned to understand eschatology existentially from within. Thus Jesus, rather than becoming a liability to modern theology, has become the inescapable factor forcing almost every modern theology into some positive relationship to eschatology. Jesus' theology is anything but irrelevant or meaningless for theological thought today. It is clear that neither of the most striking conclusions of Schweitzer's work was such as to explain why the quest of the historical Jesus came largely to an end a generation or more ago.

The real cause behind the end of the quest is to be found in a series of basic shifts which were taking place in New Testament scholarship at the opening of the century. These shifts when taken together formed a decisive cleft between nineteenth- and twentieth-century scholarship, and indicated the *impossibility* and *illegitimacy* of the quest of the historical Jesus. It is to these factors that we consequently turn.

C. THE SOURCES AND THE 'IMPOSSIBILITY' OF THE ORIGINAL QUEST

The *possibility* of the original quest resided primarily in its view of the oldest sources as the same kind of objective, positivistic historiography which the nineteenth century itself aspired to write. The basic reorientation consisted in the discovery that the Gospels are the devotional literature of the primitive Church, rather than the products of scholarship. Thus the function which the tradition about Jesus performed in the life and worship of the Church came to be recognized as the organizing principle in the formation of the individual stories and sayings, and in the formation of the Gospels themselves. This insight, already at home in Old Testament research, was carried over to the New Testament by Wellhausen. The Gospels are primary sources for the history of the early Church, and only secondarily sources for the history of Jesus.[1] Consequently the *Sitz im Leben* of each tradition must be first identified, as the key to the direction in which the tradition would be inclined to develop. Only by discounting this tendency can one then hope to disengage the oldest level in the tradition, and thus come to speak about Jesus of Nazareth in distinction from the Church's kerygmatic presentation of him. This basic methodological insight was implemented by the results of detailed analysis: William Wrede[2] demonstrated that Mark is not writing with the objectivity or even the interests of a modern historian, but rather as a theologian of the 'Messianic secret'. Karl Ludwig Schmidt[3] demonstrated that the order of events in the Gospels is not based upon a memory of the order of Jesus'

[1]This particular formulation was used by Wellhausen of Mark 8–10 and Q, but is sufficiently characteristic of his whole position in his *Einleitung in die drei ersten Evangelien* (1906, 2nd ed. 1911) to serve Bultmann ('The New Approach to the Synoptic Problem', *The Journal of Religion* VI, 1926, 341) as a summary of Wellhausen's whole position.

[2]*Das Messiasgeheimnis in den Evangelien,* 1901.

[3]*Der Rahmen der Geschichte Jesu,* 1919.

public ministry inherent in the material, but rather is largely the contribution of the redactional process, which assembled unrelated stories, sayings, and small individual collections for devotional purposes, and then arranged them topically or theologically without any serious interest in chronology or geography. The basic theses of these works have not been disproved, and therefore must continue to be presupposed in current scholarship conversant with them.

It is often assumed that the original quest came to an end in Germany because of the rise of form criticism. Since form criticism has been widely rejected in the English-speaking world, the inference is readily drawn that the original quest can properly continue untroubled.[1] However the basic assumption is in error. It was not form criticism, but rather the revolution in the generation preceding form criticism, which brought the original quest to an end. Form criticism was an outstanding attempt to implement some of those insights, but they themselves are more basic and have proved to be more lasting that has form criticism itself.

The form critic conjectured that one way to identify the *Sitz im Leben* of the gospel tradition would be to classify the material on purely formal grounds, and then to identify the function in the Church's life responsible for the rise of each identified form. This procedure is methodologically sound, but did not in practice arrive at ultimately conclusive results. This was due to the indistinctness of the formal structure of much of the material, and the difficulty of making a clear correlation between formal tendencies and their setting in the Church's life. Consequently when the form critics came to discuss the historicity of the gospel tradition, a question for which their method was at best only indirectly relevant, they tended to arrive at the conclusion which their general orientation suggested, rather than a conclusion which

[1]Vincent Taylor (*ExpT* LIII, 1941–2, 61 f.) cites rejections of form criticism by F. C. Burkitt, F. W. Howard, A. H. McNeile, and C. H. Dodd, and then remarks: 'Important, however, as these judgements are, they are opinions and no more. No one has built upon them. The universities of Great Britain are silent.'

form criticism as such required. Thus their views as to the material's historicity ranged from the more conservative position of Albertz to the mediating position of Dibelius and the radical position of Bultmann.[1] A second consequence of the inconclusiveness of the results of form criticism is that the mention of their 'forms' has largely passed out of the scholarly discussion of gospel passages, even in Germany. Thus one may say that form criticism, as applied to the gospel tradition, has to a large extent passed out of vogue. Yet it is all the more striking that the basic orientation with regard to the Gospels, of which form criticism was but one manifestation, continues as the basis of twentieth-century scholarship.

This basic reorientation is to the effect that *all* the tradition about Jesus survived only in so far as it served some function in the life and worship of the primitive Church. History survived only as *kerygma*. It is this insight which reversed our understanding of the scholar's situation with regard to the relation of factual detail and theological interpretation in the gospels. If the nineteenth century presupposed the detailed historicity of the Synoptic Gospels except where 'doctrinal tampering' was so obvious as to be inescapable (they had in mind such things as 'Paulinisms' and the miraculous), the twentieth century presupposes the kerygmatic nature of the Gospels, and feels really confident in asserting the historicity of its details only where their origin cannot be ex-

[1] Vincent Taylor (*The Formation of the Gospel Tradition*, 1933, vi) pointed out that the negative results often held to inhere in form criticism are 'not the necessary trend of the method; on the contrary, when its limitations are recognized, Form-Criticism seems . . . to furnish constructive suggestions which in many ways confirm the historical trustworthiness of the Gospel tradition.' Similarly F. C. Grant observes in his review of Dibelius' *Die Botschaft von Jesus Christus* (*Anglican Theol. Review* XVIII, 1936, 103): 'Form-Criticism has not done away with our knowledge of the historical Jesus; on the contrary, it has brought him and the earliest body of his followers far closer to us than ever before.' Cf. also M. M. Parvis, 'NT Criticism in the World-Wars Period', in *The Study of the Bible Today and Tomorrow* (ed. by Harold R. Willoughby, 1947), esp. pp. 61–68. Jeremias ('Der gegenwartige Stand der Debatte um das Problem des historischen Jesus', 168) lists form criticism among the better equipment we now have for a quest, and states: 'It is much too little known and observed that the essential significance of form criticism is that it aids us in removing a Hellenistic layer which had placed itself over the older Palestinian tradition.'

plained in terms of the life of the Church.[1] In the nineteenth century the burden of proof lay upon the scholar who saw theological interpolations in historical sources; in the twentieth century the burden of proof lies upon the scholar who sees objective factual source material in the primitive Church's book of common worship. The result is obvious: the burden of proof has shifted over to the person who maintains the possibility of the quest. This situation does not necessitate the further inference that such a quest is impossible; but it does explain how such a position seemed from a scholarly point of view 'safest', easiest to defend.

D. THE KERYGMA AND THE 'ILLEGITIMACY' OF THE ORIGINAL QUEST

If we wished to summarize in one word these considerations which led to the view that the quest was impossible, we could speak of the discovery of the *kerygma* at the centre of the Gospels. It is only here that we reach the unifying factor in all the elements bringing the quest to an end. For as a matter of fact the discovery of the *kerygma* had an even more pervasive effect upon our problem than has been stated thus far. The *kerygma* came gradually to be recognized as the centre not only of the Gospels, but also of primitive Christianity itself. Furthermore it has increasingly come to replace the theological centrality of the 'historical Jesus' in leading theological systems of our day. It was this rise of the

[1]Cf. my discussion of the resultant methodological difficulties, 'The Historical Jesus and the Church's Kerygma', *Religion in Life* XXVI, 1956-7, 40–49. The broad effect of this methodological aspect can be seen from the quotation by Vincent Taylor (*ExpT* LIII, 1941-2, 60 f.) of the method proposed by S. J. Case in his *Jesus—A New Biography*, 1927, 115: 'Every statement in the records is to be judged by the degree of its suitableness to the distinctive environment of Jesus, on the one hand, and to that of the framers of Gospel tradition at one or another stage in the history of Christianity on the other.' Taylor draws the obvious inference: 'It is not surprising that, with such a test as "our safest guide", the results were extremely meagre.' T. W. Manson observes (*ExpT* LIII, 1941-2, 249: 'Of any story or teaching we may ask concerning its "Sitz im Leben"—is it a "Sitz im Leben Jesu" or a "Sitz im Leben der alten Kitche"? It is sometimes overlooked that an affirmative answer to the latter alternative does not automatically carry with it a negative answer to the former.' This is of course correct; but Manson himself has failed to observe that it does automatically shift the burden of proof: since the historian now works backward from the date of composition rather

kerygma to the centre of our understanding of primitive Christianity, and to the normative position in contemporary theology, which was the underlying cause for questioning even the *legitimacy* of the original quest. It is this second aspect of the role of the *kerygma* in the problem of the historical Jesus which still remains to be examined in some detail.

If the nineteenth-century view of history found its meaningful expression in 'the historical Jesus', the twentieth century has found its approach to history already anticipated in the *kerygma*. We have already noted how the positivistic understanding of history as consisting of brute facts gave way to an understanding of history centring in the profound intentions, stances, and concepts of existence held by persons in the past, as the well-springs of their outward actions. Historical methodology shifted accordingly from a primary concern for recording the past 'wie es eigentlich gewesen', i.e. cataloguing with objective detachment facts in sequence and with proper casual relationships. Instead, the historian's task was seen to consist in understanding those deeply-lying intentions of the past, by involving one's selfhood in an encounter in which one's own intentions and views of existence are put in question, and perhaps altered or even radically reversed. Now the *kerygma* is formally analogous to this new approach to the historian's task, for it consists in an initial understanding of the deeper meaning of Jesus. Therefore the *kerygma*,

---

than forward from Jesus' lifetime in his search for a historical 'cause' of the material before him, the detection of such a sufficient 'cause' in the life of the Church would place the burden of proof upon the person who wished to affirm the existence of another 'cause' of the item under consideration lying still farther back, i.e. back in the life of Jesus. For an acute formulation of these difficulties within the context of the new quest cf. Käsemann, ZTK LI, 1954, 144: 'We wish to characterize the embarrassment of critical research only in a few rough lines: the historical reliability of the synoptic tradition has become doubtful all along the line; yet for working out the authentic material going back to Jesus we are largely lacking in an essential presupposition, namely a survey of the earliest stage of the primitive Church, and are almost completely lacking in sufficient and valid criteria. Only in one single case do we have relatively firm ground under our feet, namely when for some reason a tradition can neither be derived from Judaism nor attributed to primitive Christianity, and especially when Jewish Christianity has toned down or bent the material it received as too daring.'

rather than brute facts of Jesus' external biography, was identified as our primary historical source for understanding his meaning. Of course this does not mean that the historian automatically accepts the *kerygma* as the correct interpretation of Jesus' meaning, for it, like any other interpretation, is subject to critical re-examination. But it does mean that we have moved beyond the initial conclusion that the kerygmatized Gospels are incompatible with the historian's objectives, to the recognition that they in their way are doing something similar to what the modern historian in his way would like to do.

Just as the *kerygma* provided a *rapprochement* to the current view of history and historiography, it also provided the unifying factor between the twentieth-century reconstruction of primitive Christianity and its own systematic theological reflection. This becomes apparent when one scans the interrelated course of New Testament research and systematic thought in this century. The century opened with the older generation still following the Ritschlian approach to God in terms of ethical idealism,[1] and to Jesus as the historical fact exemplifying that ideal. However Ritschlianism was already giving way to the *religionsgeschichtliche Schule*, whose philosophy of religion centred in a decided preference for cultic experience over ethical action, and whose historical reconstruction saw primitive Christianity orientated like other Hellenistic religions to the cult's dying and rising Lord, rather than to the Jesus of the Sermon on the Mount. This school combined its theological and historical positions into the normative statement that Christianity centres in a numinous experience of the dying and rising Lord, not in the ethical experience of the historical Jesus. Christ the

[1]This neo-Kantian background of Ritschlianism became explicit as early as Wilhelm Herrmann's *Die Religion im Verhaltnis zum Welterkennen und zur Sittlichkeit*, 1879, which marked the shift away from the basis of the mediating theology in idealistic metaphysics to the neo-Kantian connexion of religion with ethics (cf. my work *Das Problem des Heiligen Geistes bei Wilhelm Herrmann*, 1952). This union is still a commonplace at the end of the Ritschlian period, e.g. in Harnack's position in his debate with Barth of 1923 (cf. Vol. 3 of Barth's collected essays, *Theologische Fragen und Antworten*, 1957, 8): 'If God and world (life in God and worldly life) are absolute contradictions, how is education to God, i.e. to the good, possible? But how is education possible without historical knowledge and high esteem of morality?'

Lord is the cult symbol of Christianity, but it would be an instance of the genetic fallacy to concern oneself with problems related to the historical origin of that symbol, i.e. its relation to the historical Jesus.

Between the wars the *religionsgeschichtliche Schule* faded away, and its historical reconstruction underwent a transformation in terms of more current theological orientations. The emphasis of comparative religion on the point that primitive Christianity centred in a dying and rising divinity was subsequently transformed, for instance by C. H. Dodd, into the emphasis on the point that the original *kerygma* had at its centre Christ's death and resurrection. And under Barthian influence, Rudolf Otto's 'numinous' experience of the *tremendum* and *fascinans* was clarified as an existential encounter with the proclamation of Jesus' death and resurrection, i.e. as judgement and grace.[1] Thus the *kerygma* became recognized as central in both senses of the term: as the content of the message and as the act of preaching.[2]

[1]This is e.g. the avenue by which Bultmann shifted from the comparative religious school into the contemporary discussion. Cf. *GuV* I, 22, and his review of Barth's *Romans*, *ChrW* XXXVI, 1922, 320.

[2]C. F. Evans, 'The Kerygma', *JTS*, n.s. VII, 1956, 26, in his polemic against Dodd's view, attempts to eliminate from the NT the usage of κήρυγμα to designate the content of the message. The same thesis is presented over against Bultmann by Kurt Goldammer, 'Der *Kerygma*-Begriff in der ältesten christlichen Literatur', *ZNTW* XLVIII, 1957, 80 f. However the complete elimination of the meaning 'content of the message' cannot be carried through in I Cor. 1.21, in view of the context, vv. 18, 23 (cf. G. Friedrich in *TWNT* III, 715). It is true that the same term is used in 2.4 to designate the act of preaching, rather than the content. But it becomes unnecessary to harmonize the meaning in 1.21 with that of 2.4, once one has recognized that Paul is in 2.4 (as frequently elsewhere) applying the *content* of the *kerygma* (repeated in 2.2) to his own existence, in this case his existence as *preacher* (cf. an existential application already in 1.26–31). Thus the use of the two meanings of the term in one context (1.21; 2.4) is due to Paul's recognizing that the past action of God in Christ (the content of the *kerygma*) recurs in his presence existence (the act of preaching). Of course it is of considerably more importance than debating the NT usage of the term, to recognize that the *kerygma* of primitive Christianity, whatever they may or may not have called it, did have in it these two aspects of 'recital of past event' and 'recurrence of present event'. This point is well made by William Baird, 'What is the Kerygma? A Study of I Cor. 15.3–8 and Gal. 1.11–17', *JBL* LXXVI, 1957, 181–91. Much the same point with regard to the tradition had already been made by Oscar Cullmann, 'The Tradition', in *The Early Church*, 55–99, a reprint of his article '*Kyrios* as Designation for the Oral Tradition concerning

These two aspects of the term correspond respectively to the contemporary historical reconstruction of primitive Christianity and to the normative centre of contemporary theology, so that the term *kerygma* comes to represent the unifying element in the contemporary situation: historically speaking, the central content of primitive Christian preaching was God's eschatological action centring in the saving event of cross and resurrection. Theologically speaking, this saving event proclaimed by the *kerygma* shows itself to be eschatological precisely by recurring in the proclamation of the *kerygma* itself: the act of proclaiming Jesus' death and resurrection becomes God's act calling upon me to accept my death and receive resurrected life.[1] Believing the witness about God's past action in Christ coincides with the occur-

---

Jesus (*Paradosis* and *Kyrios*)', *Scottish Journal of Theology* III, 1950, 180–97 (cf. my review, *JBL* LXXV, 1956, 238–9).

[1]The coinciding of the witness to past event with the present recurrence of the event in Paul's theology has been worked out by Bultmann (*Theology of the New Testament* I, 292 ff.), who presents this as basic to the whole biblical concept of the Word of God (*GuV* I, 287 f.): '*Thus the relation to history is a constitutive character of the Word of God in the OT.* And whatever historical events may be named, irrespective of whether one's fantasy moves *via* the delivery from Egypt back even to patriarchal times, or whether God's acts in the most recent past are named, history is conceived of as a unity, as unified action of God, out of which each Now arises, and which gives to each Now and thus to each Word of God spoken to Now its character. In this sense *the Word as call* (for decision) *is at the same time communication* (of information), and both form a unity, since what is communicated, *the history, itself calls in the Now.* Consequently obedient submission under the Word encountered now is at the same time faithfulness to what God did to the people and thus to the individual. *Faith is obedience, which is at the same time faithfulness and trust.* Thus the communicating of the past does not have the meaning of a historical report, but rather is a call, in which the past is contemporized. The contemporizing of history takes place neither in poetic recollection, nor in scholarly reconstruction, but rather in a calling tradition, in which the history itself "becomes vocal", becomes the Word.' A remarkably similar position as to the nature of history is taken by R. G. Collingwood (*The Idea of History*, 1946, 158): 'The historian, if he thinks his past is a dead past, is certainly making a mistake; but Oakeshott (*Experience and its Modes*, 1933, 111) supposes that there is no third alternative to the disjunction that the past is either a dead past or not past at all but simply present. The third alternative is that it should be a living past, a past which, because it was thought and not mere natural event, can be re-enacted in the present and in that re-enactment known as past.' Cf. also paragraph 76 of Martin Heidegger's *Sein und Zeit*, 1927: 'Der existenziale Ursprung der Historie aus der Geschichtlichkeit des Daseins.'

rence of this divine action in my present life. Herein resides the
unity of God's action in history, and ultimately the meaningfulness of the Trinity. Thus both as witness to past event and as
experience of present event, the *kerygma* is central in primitive
Christianity and contemporary theology. It is for this reason that
the *kerygma* has become a whole unified theological position
which has just as nearly swept the field in twenticth-century
theology as did the theology of the historical Jesus in the nineteenth century.

The historian's detection of the *kerygma* at the centre of the
Gospels found a formal analogy in the contemporary view of
historiography as concerned with underlying meaning, and this
correlation led to the view that the kind of quest of the historical
Jesus envisaged by the nineteenth century not only *cannot* succeed, but is hardly appropriate to the intention of the Gospels and
the goal of modern historiography. The theologian's recognition
that the *kerygma* provides the normative pattern of contemporary
religious experience also found a formal analogy in the contemporary view of existence, and it is *this* correlation which gave
impetus to the view that the kind of quest which the nineteenth
century envisaged *ought not* to succeed.

Christianity began with the call of the eschatological *kerygma*
to break with the 'present evil aeon' and to commit oneself
existentially to the 'aeon to come', which has drawn so near as
to be already the horizon of present existence (e.g. Matt. 4.17;
Rom. 12.2). God's judgement upon this world must be accepted
as God's judgement upon myself, while the kingdom breaking in
and destroying the present evil aeon is accepted as the grace of
God in my life. Thus the *kerygma* proclaims the death in which
resides life (Mark 8.35), a *kerygma* incarnated in Jesus and therefore shifting terminologically from Jesus' own eschatological
message into the Church's christological *kerygma*: this death in
which life resides is Jesus' death, and becomes available only in
dying and rising with him. This meant for the earliest disciples
a basic renunciation of the struggle for existence, implemented
by a complete break with the power structure of society: the

automatic prerogatives of the chosen people, the security of the holy tradition, the comfort of established religious organization and clergy—all such props, controlled by man and as a result constantly available to him for securing his existence, were in principle eliminated. Judaism's 'confidence in the flesh' was revealed as the basic rebellion of the *homo religiosus* against God (e.g. Phil. 3; Rom. 10.3). Man must build his existence upon that which is beyond his control and available only as God's gift (*ubi et quando visum est deo*), upon a world which is transcendent by being basically future, and present only as the eschatological miracle, the gift of transcendence. Thus 'faith', the pattern of contemporary religious experience which is to relate us to God through Christ, cannot by its very nature be built upon 'the present evil aeon', with all that it provides of worldly security under man's control and invariably at his disposai; by definition 'faith' is the life given in death, and consequently has its basis beyond our control, is lived out of the future, is 'an act of faith'.

Now it became increasingly clear that 'the historical Jesus', the scholarly reconstruction of Jesus' biography by means of objective historical method, was just such an attempt to build one's existence upon that which is under man's control and invariably at his disposal. The historical Jesus as a proven divine fact is a worldly security with which the *homo religiosus* arms himself in his effort to become self-sufficient before God, just as did the Jew in Paul's day by appeal to the law. Whereas the *kerygma* calls for existential commitment to the meaning of Jesus, the original quest was an attempt to avoid the risk of faith by supplying objectively verified proof for its 'faith'. To require an objective legitimization of the saving event prior to faith is to take offence at the offence of Christianity and to perpetuate the unbelieving flight to security, i.e. the reverse of faith. For faith involves the rejection of worldly security as righteousness by works. Thus one has come to recognize the worldliness of the 'historicism' and 'psychologism' upon which the original quest was built. To this extent the original quest came to be regarded as theologically illegitimate.

The classical document for this radical shift in the theological appraisal of the quest is the debate in 1923 between Harnack and Barth.[1] For Harnack, the 'content of the gospel' consisted in concepts which must be disengaged from the historical ambiguities of the Bible and then grasped intellectually, a task which can only be performed by 'historical knowledge and critical reflection'. This same rationalistic approach to the gospel was applied to the believer's knowledge of Jesus: 'If the person of Jesus Christ stands at the centre of the gospel, how can the basis for a reliable and communal knowledge of this person be gained other than through critical historical study, if one is not to trade a dreamed up Christ for the real one? But how is this study to be made except by scholarly theology?' To this Barth replied: 'The reliability and communal nature of the knowledge of the person of Jesus Christ as the centre of the *gospel* can be no other than the reliability and communal nature of the *faith* awakened by God. Critical historical study signifies the deserved and necessary end of those 'bases' of such knowledge which are no bases since they are not laid by God himself. The man who does not yet know (and that *still* means all of us) that we know Christ *no* longer according to the flesh, can learn it from critical biblical scholarship: the more radically he is shocked, the better it is both for him and for the cause. And this may then perhaps be the service which "historical knowledge" can perform for the real task of theology.' Barth's basic position was that the 'theme of theology' is 'God's revelation', rather than any given concepts in the history of ideas. Consequently the fundamental role of historical critical scholarship would be quite different from that which Harnack conceived it to be: 'Historical knowledge could then of course say that the communicating of the "content of the gospel", at least according to its own statement, can be carried out only by an action of this "content" *himself*. "Critical reflection" could lead to the result that this statement made by the gospel is based in the

[1]In *Die Christliche Welt,* reprinted in the third volume of Barth's *Gesammelte Vorträge* which is entitled *Theologische Fragen und Antworten,* 1957, 'Ein Briefwechsel mit Adolf von Harnack', 7–31.

nature of the case (the relation between God and man), and consequently is to be seriously respected.' Bultmann[1] promptly shifted away from liberalism to the position of Barth, and the rejection of the quest on theological grounds gradually became a commonplace of contemporary theology.

Now the theological considerations leading to the rejection of the original quest as illegitimate correspond formally to the general pattern of existentialistic thought in our day. For existentialism usually conceives of inauthentic existence as man's attempt to avoid the 'awful freedom' of his historicity, and to find security in his human nature, which is understood quite rationalistically: the individual is a particular, comfortably subsumed under a universal. Inauthentic existence is a life built upon conformity, the herd instinct, the tradition, that which is objectively available and controllable. The original quest was thus one way of implementing such a proclivity toward inauthentic existence.[2]

This is not to say that authentic existence as understood by existentialism is materially the same as eschatological existence, but only that there is a formal analogy. For both viewpoints authentic existence is selfhood constituted by commitment, and consists in constant *engagement*. The nature of the commitment can vary as sharply as do Faust and Jesus; the 'world' in which one is *engagé* can vary as radically as do 'the present evil aeon' and the kingdom of God. The formal analogy affects the substance at

[1]'Die liberale Theologie und die jüngste theologische Bewegung', *TB* III, 1924, 73–86, reprinted in *GuV* I, 1–25. For this specific point cf. p. 3 f.

[2]Martin Heidegger, *Sein und Zeit*, 1927, 395: 'The question as to whether history has as its object the listing of unique, "individual" affairs or also "laws" has already gone astray at the root. The theme of history is neither the purely unique occurrence nor some generality floating above it, but rather the possibility which was factually existent. This is not reproduced as such, i.e. really understood historically, when it is perverted into the pallor of a supra-historical pattern. Only factual authentic historicity, as determined fate, is able so to open up the history which has been, that in the repetition the "power" of the possible strikes into one's factual existence, i.e. comes to it as its futurity. . . . In no science are the "universal validity" of the standards and the claims of "universality" which the impersonal "one" and its common sense requires, *less* possible criteria of "truth" than in authentic history.'

only one point: a Christian content without the form of commitment and *engagement* becomes a this-worldly Christendom at ease in Zion, a dead orthodoxy, a white-washed tomb, a tinkling cymbal, and ceases really to be the Christian content. A Jesus whose role is established in terms of this world is not the eschatological Messiah transcending this world.

This formal analogy between Christian existence and existentialism draws attention to another aspect of 'historicism' which is theologically illegitimate. Sometimes historical critical scholars absolutized their method of objectivity into a permanent avoidance of existential encounter with the history they were supposedly studying. But existentialism insists that one should be *engagé*, with one's whole selfhood at stake, in the 'world' in which one moves. And the *kerygma* calls for a total encounter with the person of Jesus, in which the self is put in radical decision. Therefore it can only regard as illegitimate a scholarly career which becomes in the long run no more than a distracting fascination with historical details about Jesus, details which may occupy the memory, move the emotions, prod the conscience, or stimulate the intellect, but fail to put the self in radical decision. This insight in no sense invalidated the role of detailed and exacting research. But it did mean that the historian's personal authenticity could not be found in increasingly narrowed specialization; rather this came to be recognized as an escape mechanism in a situation where one's research had actually become existentially meaningless. Thus both forms which the historical study of Jesus took at the opening of the century—the attempt to prove historically his absoluteness, and the ultimate lack of interest in him as a possible understanding of one's own existence, came to be recognized as illegitimate. In each of these various ways the temper of our day united with the course of theological and historical reflection to bring the quest of the historical Jesus to an end.

47

III

THE POSSIBILITY OF A NEW QUEST

If the rise of the *kerygma* meant that we cannot and ought not continue the quest of the historical Jesus, any reappraisal of the problem must concentrate upon these two aspects. Therefore we first inquire as to whether we *can* renew the quest of the historical Jesus.

A. THE 'HISTORICAL SECTION' OF THE KERYGMA?

The more one catches sight of the decisive role the *kerygma* played in bringing the quest to an end, the more one recognizes the relevance of C. H. Dodd's attempt to show that the *kerygma* contained something corresponding to a life of Jesus, namely a sketch of the public ministry.[1] However his competent presentation only served to show the difficulties inherent in such an avenue toward reconciling the *kerygma* and the quest of the historical Jesus.

First of all, he neglected the fact that the *kerygma* receives its tremendous authority in theology today not simply from its position in the history of ideas, i.e. not simply as precedent, but rather from its existential function as a call to faith, in which God calls upon me to accept his judgement upon me in Jesus' death, and to live from his grace in Jesus' resurrection. Even if the *kerygma* as historical precedent contained details of Jesus' bio-

---

[1] The relevance of his attempt is evident, e.g. from the following statement by Hermann Diem, *Theologie* II, 78: 'The life and preaching of the historical Jesus are available for us only in the post-Easter *kerygma*, and are so covered over by it that it is impossible to reconstruct out of it again a history of Jesus. The Synoptics are of course of the opinion that they are giving historical factual reports, although measured by our modern meaning of history they operate in a naïvely uncritical way. But their reporting exclusively served the *kergyma*, which concentrated on cross and resurrection.'

graphy, just as it contained at times mythological motifs from Hellenistic syncretism, the *kerygma* as eschatological event does not impose upon me the thought patterns with which it originally operated. For Dodd's approach to succeed, it would be necessary to show that the inclusion of details from Jesus' life is not part of the *adiaphora*, i.e. not just one means among others of emphasizing the incarnation, but rather that it is indispensable for conveying the existential meaning of the *kerygma*, i.e. is constitutive of the *kerygma* as eschatological event. This is difficult in view of the fact that apart from Acts the *kerygma* is almost totally lacking in biographical facts, and that in Acts the facts listed vary from sermon to sermon.[1]

The way in which Dodd attempts to reconcile the *kerygma* and the quest is in the second place misleading, since it interprets the 'historical section of the *kerygma*' (47)[2] in terms of a positivistic view of history, rather than in terms of the theological approach to history which actually characterized primitive Christianity. For Dodd characterizes this 'historical section' as presenting the 'historical facts of the life of Jesus' (31), a 'comprehensive summary of the facts of the ministry of Jesus' (28), so that the average reader would be misled into the assumption that the *kerygma* was concerned with the objectively verifiable 'data' (29) of the historian. To begin with, this language suggests considerably more 'data' than are actually to be found in the rather meagre factual detail of the sermons in Acts, not to speak of the almost complete absence of such detail in kerygmatic texts outside Acts. But even more important, the direction in which this 'historical section' is interpreted is in terms of the *Sitz im Leben* of the historian, rather than

---

[1]Somewhat analogous is the widespread modern viewpoint that certain facts are essential to the *kerygma*, and an almost equally widespread dissensus as to which these essential facts are. This point has been made by William Baird (*JBL* LXXVI, 1957, 182), who points to this discrepancy within the agreement of A. Hunter, C. T. Craig, F. V. Filson, T. F. Glasson, and B. Gärtner. E. L. Allen, 'The Lost Kerygma', *New Testament Studies* III, 1957, 349–53, has shown that the most impressive list of facts in the *kerygma*, the list of appearances in I Cor. 15.3 ff., seems to have been largely 'lost' prior to the writing of the resurrection narratives of the Gospels.

[2]Numbers refer to pages of *The Apostolic Preaching and its Development*, 1936, 2nd ed. 1944.

in terms of the *Sitz im Leben* of the primitive Christian. It may be that kerygmatic allusions to Jesus' humility, meekness, gentleness, love, forgiveness and obedience derive from historical memory of Jesus;[1] but the 'historical value' which such material may have is far from its kerygmatic meaning, which is more accurately stated by Bultmann, in language actually intended to state the significance of the pre-existence in the *kerygma*: 'That Jesus, the historical person, did this service for us, and that he did it not out of personal sympathy and loveableness, but rather by God acting in him, in that God established his love for us through Jesus dying for us sinners (Rom. 5.6–8).'[2]

One need only read the kerygmatic hymn in Phil. 2.6–11 to see the role this 'historical section of the *kerygma*' originally played:

I

6 Who being in the form of God
   Did not count equality with God a thing to be grasped
7 But emptied himself,
   Taking the form of a servant.

II

Being born in the likeness of man
And being found in human form
8 He humbled himself
Becoming obedient unto death (i.e. the death of the cross).

III

9 Therefore God has highly exalted him
   And bestowed on him the name which is above every name,
10 That at the name of Jesus every knee should bow,
   (in heaven and on earth and under the earth)
11 And every tongue confess: JESUS CHRIST IS LORD
   (to the glory of God the Father).[3]

[1]So Dodd, *History and the Gospel,* 1938, Ch. II. One should observe that this possibility is far from proven by Dodd, who contents himself with the demonstration that these motifs do not derive from OT prophecy.
[2]*GuV* I, 213.
[3]This strophic arrangement was proposed by Joachim Jeremias, 'Zur Gedankenführung in den paulinischen Briefen', *Studia Paulina,* 1953, 152–4, and was accepted by Otto Michel, 'Zur Exegese von Phil. 2.5–11', *Theologie als Glaubenswagnis,* 1954, 79–95. It was arrived at independently by L. Cerfaux, 'L'hymne au Christ-Serviteur de Dieu', *Miscellanea historica in honorem Alberti de Meyer,* 1946, 117–30, although without any of Jeremias' deletions from the Pauline text.

Although no facts from Jesus' life are reported, his humiliation is emphasized as the indispensable presupposition of his exaltation. It is this meaning of humiliation which keeps the 'historical section of the *kerygma*' from attempting to legitimize the *kerygma* with objectively demonstrable 'signs'. For not only did Jesus reject such an insistence upon legitimizing signs, but Paul explicitly recognized the rejection of such signs as inherent in the existential meaning of the *kerygma* (I Cor. 1.17–25).[1] Consequently when details do on occasion come to be introduced into the 'historical section of the *kerygma*', the normative significance of their introduction should not be seen in terms of positivistic historiography. Rather is it necessary to seek to trace the original kerygmatic meaning at work in this procedure, in order to reach a valid kerygmatic approach to the Gospels and a normative basis for a modern quest of the historical Jesus.

The central strophe in the hymn of Phil. 2.6–11 presents Jesus' earthly life in the lowest possible terms,[2] precisely because the first strophe about the Pre-existent[3] and the third strophe about

[1] An interesting parallel is to be found in the case of Paul's discussion of the 'signs' legitimizing himself, in II Cor. 10–13. Here he begins by listing facts which positively demonstrate his superiority—but all under the admission 'I am speaking as a fool', i.e. such a method is contrary to the *kerygma*. Then he shifts to speaking paradoxically of his humiliation, as the only Christian way of speaking of one's own history.

[2] Käsemann, 'Kritische Analyse von Phil. 2.5–11', *ZTK* XLVII, 1950, 334 ff., rightly accentuates this aspect of the hymn.

[3] Cf. Bultmann, *GuV* I, 213: 'That Jesus, the historical person, did this service for us (sc. of renewing us to a new understanding of ourselves in obedience and love), and that he did it not out of personal sympathy and loveableness, but rather by God acting in him, in that God established his love for us through Jesus dying for us sinners (Rom. 5.6–8)—that is the meaning of language about the Preexistent.' *Kerygma and Myth*, 35: 'Our interest in the events of his life, and above all in the cross, is more than an academic concern with the history of the past. We can see meaning in them only when we ask what God is trying to say to each one of us through them. Again, the figure of Jesus cannot be understood simply from his context in human evolution or history. In mythological language, this means that he stems from eternity, his origin transcends both history and nature.' One may question whether, with Jeremias, the whole of strophe I in Phil. 2.6–11 treats of the Pre-existent, or whether, with Käsemann (*ZTK* XLVII, 1950, 334 ff.), incarnation is not rather already involved in the last half of strophe I.

the Exalted[1] point to the meaningfulness of his (and therefore our) very ambiguous historical existence. Although pre-existence and exaltation are, so to speak, chronologically separate from the life, they reveal the life's whence and whither, and are thus a way of expressing its meaning. This method is quite common in kerygmatic texts of the briefer 'humiliation—exaltation' type (Rom. 1.3-4; I Tim. 3.16; I Peter 3.18b), as well as in kerygmatic texts with much the same 'pre-existence—humiliation—exaltation' pattern as Phil. 2.6-11 (e.g. Col. 1.15-20; Heb. 1.2 ff.; II Cor. 8.9; Rom. 10.6-9; I Cor. 8.6). Even though the 'historical section' or humiliation seems even to disappear from some of these kerygmatic texts, their original intention was to emphasize the meaningfulness of Jesus' historicity or humiliation, and only with gnosticism was this original meaning lost.

Consequently the introduction of details into the 'historical section of the *kerygma*' is valid only[2] as an impressive way of witnessing to this kerygmatic message, that in suffering lies glory, in death resides life, in judgement is to be found grace. Whereas the *kerygma* customarily describes this 'exaltation to be found in humiliation' by stating the exaltation *outside* the 'historical section', sometimes the *kerygma* superimposes the exaltation *upon* the

[1]Lohmeyer, *Kyrios Jesus. Eine Untersuchung zu Phil.* 2.5-11, 1928, 56: 'The name Jesus seems to have been chosen in order to remain in the realm of the historical.' Käsemann (*ZTK* XLVII, 1950, 354) locates the same emphasis in the meaning of the whole hymn: 'The scope of the whole, according to the analysis here carried through, is: the obedient one is the Cosmocrator. As such he is criterion and κριτής of all history. In the last judgement there stands only this theme for discussion, whether we were obedient or not. . . . This distinguishes the Christian *kerygma* from myth, that the obedient one, and he alone, determines the cosmos and its history in this way. And what is meant here by obedience has become clear from the interpretation of vv. 7-8, namely this, that lowliness is laid hold of as the possibility of freedom. The myth, which was and is always interested in apotheosis, never proclaimed this. Here is its limit, and here it is demonstrated that the primitive Christian message is only making use for its own purposes of the myth's categories.'

[2]Cf. the *Sachkritik* advocated here by Bultmann (*GuV* I, 54; *Kerygma and Myth*, 112; *Theology of the New Testament* I, 295) with regard to I Cor. 15.5, and by Ernst Haenchen (*Die Apostelgeschichte*, 1956, 154) with regard to Acts 2.22. For a divergent exegesis of I Cor. 15.5 cf., in addition to Karl Barth, *The Resurrection of the Dead*, 1933, 131 ff.: Ernst Fuchs, *Hermeneutik*, 1954, 185, and *ZTK* LIII, 1956, 212. Cf. also Diem's attempt to mediate, *Theologie* II, 112 f.

humiliation, so that life becomes visible *in* death, glory *in* suffering, grace *in* judgement, the exaltation *in* the humiliation, the resurrection glory *in* the 'historical section'. The statements about Jesus 'in the flesh', originally intended to designate only the humiliation half of the paradox, come to express both sides of it. 'Put to death in the flesh' (I Peter 3.18) becomes *'Revealed* in the flesh' (I Tim. 3.16).[1] And the statement of Jesus' this-worldly origin 'according to the flesh' is not only *followed* by a statement about his other-worldly origin 'according to the Spirit', but also includes *within* the this-worldly side an allusion to the messianic lineage (Rom. 1.3; 9.5; Ignatius, *Smyrn.* 1.1), so that both sides of the paradox are present within the 'historical section'.[2] Another expression for Jesus' this-worldly origin is 'born of a woman' (Gal. 4.4), and this too comes to express both sides of the paradox, in the expression 'born of a virgin' (Ignatius, *Smyrn.* 1.1, Justin, *Dial.* 85.2; *Apol.* 31.7; 32.14).[3]

Now this trend within the kerygmatic tradition is the move-

[1]Yet the lowly half of the paradox is still retained, in that the line presents a contrasting pair to the exaltation line: 'Justified in the Spirit'. For the antithetic structure of the whole cf. Eduard Schweizer, *Erniedrigung und Erhöhung bei Jesus und seinen Nachfolgern,* 1955, 63–66; *TWNT* VI, 414. The shift from 'put to death' to 'revealed' may be due to the influence of the kerygmatic type designated by N. A. Dahl ('Formgeschichtliche Beobachtungen zur Christusverkündigung in der Gemeindepredigt', *Neutestamentliche Studien für Rudolf Bultmann, ZNTW,* Beiheft 21, 1954, 4 f.) as 'revelation-pattern': 'present from eternity on—now revealed'. For a sub-form 'speaks of the mystery which was earlier hidden, but now has been revealed, I Cor. 2.6 ff.; Col. 1.26 f.; Eph. 3.4–7, 8–11; Rom. 16.25 f.' When one recalls (cf. Eduard Norden, *Agnostos Theos,* 1923, 255 f., nn. 5 and 6) the great similarity of I Tim. 3.16 to Rom. 16.25 f. and Col. 1.26 f., where 'revealed' also introduces the transition, the historical origin of this kerygmatic development beyond I Peter 3.18 is explained. Cf. also II *Clem.* 14.2. (An English abridgement of *Erniedrigung und Erhöhung* has appeared under the title 'Lordship and Discipleship' in the same series as the present work. Page references here are to the fuller German edition.)

[2]Eduard Schweizer, 'Röm. 1.3 f. und der Gegensatz vom Fleisch und Geist vor und bei Paulus', *EvTh* XIV, 1955, 563–71, and *Erniedrigung und Erhöhung,* 56, sees only the humiliation in the expression; cf. also *TWNT* VI, 414 f. Hans Conzelmann called my attention to the dialectic within the humiliation line itself, as a criticism of Schweizer's presentation.

[3]The lowly half of the paradox is also retained in this expression. In Ignatius, *Smyrn.* 1.1 this is evident from the addition of 'truly', which is used in the brief chapter three times to stress the reality of Jesus' humanity over against docetism. Since the immediately preceding context is a contrasting

ment which logically leads to the writing of Gospels.[1] This is most apparent in the case of the Gospel of John. For this Gospel, more self-consciously and explicitly than the others, speaks of Jesus in terms of the *kerygma*. Therefore we should not be surprised to see the Gospel of John consciously superimposing the glory of pre-existence and exaltation upon the 'historical section'. The pre-existent glory 'still' shines in the earthly life: 'The word became flesh, and dwelt among us, and we beheld his glory' (1.14). And the glory of exaltation is 'already' in the earthly life: The cross is 'already' Jesus' 'glorification' (7.39; 12.16; 13.31;

---

pair, one may recognize in the immediately following allusion to Jesus' baptism the 'exaltation' (Spirit) line corresponding to the 'humiliation' of birth, so that the 'flesh-Spirit' pattern evident in the preceding context of David and God's son is repeated of birth by Mary and baptism by the Spirit; in view of I Peter 3.18; I Tim. 3.16, one may even sense the same 'flesh-Spirit' pattern in the following context treating of death and resurrection.— In the first passage from Justin (*Dial.* 85.2), the expression 'born of a virgin' falls within the humiliation half of an a b b a pattern:

> This son of God and firstborn of all creation,
> Both born through a virgin and become passible man,
> Both crucified under Pontius Pilate by your people and killed,
> Both raised from the dead and ascended into heaven.

In the second passage (*Apol.* 31.7), 'begotten through a virgin and made man' (at the incarnation) stands in contrast to 'being and being called son of God' (at the ascension). In the third passage (*Apol.* 32.14), 'through a virgin of the seed of Jacob' stands over against 'through the power of God'.—A similar use of 'Mary' to suggest both humiliation and exaltation may be observed in Ignatius (*Eph.* 18.2):

> By Mary, according to the dispensation of God,
> Of the seed of David, and also of the Holy Spirit.

Here the virginity is clearly recognized, but is listed (19.1) with the birth and death as the mystery which remained hidden until the ascension. In *Eph.* 7.2 'both of Mary and of God' is an antithetic pair corresponding to 'both flesh and spirit, both born and not born'. 'Mary' occurs in anti-docetic polemic to emphasize Jesus' humanity in *Trall.* 9.1.

[1] Thus this discussion should serve as a contribution to the solution of a problem to which T. W. Manson called attention in his lecture on 'The Life of Jesus: A Study of the Available Materials' (*Bulletin of the John Rylands Library* XXVII, 1942–3, 337). He observes correctly that the *kerygma* makes only 'bare mention' of Jesus' ministry 'in the most general terms, without details'. Then he observes: 'Nevertheless, before the end of the first century we have gospels which offer a narrative of the Ministry. We have what Luke calls in his Preface a *diegesis* of the things that had happened, a detailed narrative that links the Ministry with the Passion. How was the transition from *kerygma* to *diegesis* made? There lies one of the most fascinating as it is one of the most vital of Gospel problems.'

17.1, 5) and 'exaltation' (3.14; 8.28; 12.32–34). Similarly the synoptic tradition embedded the exaltation within the humiliation, most clearly in the transfiguration scene, but also in Jesus' miracles, brilliant teachings, and victorious debates. And here too, just as in the case of the sermons in Acts (2.22; 10.38), the use of various Jewish and Hellenistic styles of narrating the divine in history[1] should not mislead us as to the normative kerygmatic significance which is to be maintained throughout this transition from '*kerygma*' to 'narrative'. In the narrative, just as in the *kerygma*, we are confronted with paradox: exaltation in humiliation, life in death, the kingdom of God in the present evil aeon, the eschatological in history. This kerygmatic meaning of the 'historical section' is constitutive of the Gospel as a literary form. This is apparent in Mark's 'messianic secret'[2] and finds expression in the modern definition of the Gospels as 'passion narratives with long introductions'.[3]

---

[1]Cf. e.g. the discussion of motifs in the miracle stories borrowed from the common stock of the Hellenistic world for portraying the divine man, in Dibelius' *From Tradition to Gospel*, 1934, Ch. IV.

[2]This point has been most clearly made by Hans Conzelmann (*ZTK* LIV, 1957, 293–5), in his reversal of Wrede's explanation of the Marcan 'messianic secret': Mark's 'construction consisted not in forcing unmessianic units into the christological framework of faith, but rather in taking a mass of material already understood in a christological sense and composing it according to the *kerygma* (understood in terms of the secrecy christology). The idea of the secret does not derive from historical, pragmatic considerations. Rather it expresses a positive understanding of revelation, as is apparent e.g. in the passage Mark 4.10–12, composed by Mark himself. It is not the *un*messianic character of the elements of the tradition, but rather their messianic character, which gives difficulty to the evangelist, in view of which he has trouble enough in carrying through his theological doctrine. This is apparent in the literary and even logical violence of such passages as 4.10 ff.; 8.31–33 (in view of the confession to Christ in his source!). . . . The concept of secrecy is apparently supplied by the tradition as a *theological* conception, and in turn provides the possibility of conceiving the material, in form so divergent, under one unified point of view. *The theory of secrecy is the hermeneutic presupposition of the form 'Gospel'*.

[3]Ernst Fuchs (*ZTK* LIII, 1956, 225) has amplified in a twofold sense Martin Kähler's famous definition of the Gospels as passion narratives projected back upon the public ministry. On the one hand the passion does not need to be 'projected back', for it was already in the public ministry. And on the other hand: 'The Gospels are in reality not only passion narratives, but first of all the proclamation of the resurrection, and they are this from the very beginning.'

The paradox inherent in the *kerygma* and the Gospels is beyond objective verification by the historian. Neither the *kerygma*, nor the kerygmatic Gospels, can legitimately be used to lead us into a positivistic approach to the quest of the historical Jesus.

When the emphasis laid by the *kerygma* upon the historicity or humiliation of Jesus has been misunderstood in terms of nineteenth-century historiography, it is almost inevitable that one would search in the *kerygma* for the implementation of that kind of historiography. Dodd is only carrying out this logical consequence when he seeks to find a chronology of the public ministry in the *kerygma*; and the failure of this attempt should confirm the thesis that the basic meaning of Jesus' historicity for the *kerygma* has been misunderstood. Outside Acts, the kerygmatic texts contain no factual details from the public ministry. In the sermons of Acts, the few details from the public ministry provide no chronological information. We can infer from Acts 10.37; 13.24 f. that the public ministry's beginning at John the Baptist preceded its end on the cross; but since one knows *a priori* that the beginning precedes the end, this element reflects no more chronological information or interests than does the hymn of Phil. 2.6–11, where we can infer that the incarnation preceded the death. In two sermons of Acts various elements of the public ministry are mentioned, but without chronological order: the 'mighty works and wonders and signs' of 2.22 are not different facts occurring in that order in the public ministry; the only 'order' one might sense is a certain parallel to the order in the immediately preceding prophecy from Joel 2.28–32. Acts 10.38 says that Jesus 'went about doing good and healing all that were oppressed by the devil, for God was with him'. This Lucan formulation includes no chronological sequence; or should we assume that 'doing good' refers to one phase of the public ministry, which was then followed by another, in which 'doing good' was superseded by exorcisms? If so, one would then arrive at the reverse of the Marcan order!

The complete absence from the *kerygma* of a chronology for the public ministry should have been sufficient evidence to indicate that the kind of historicity in which the *kerygma* was interested differed basically from that with which Dodd was occupied. But it is indicative of Dodd's intellectual stature that he nonetheless carried through the logic of his position, and does actually present us with a kerygmatic chronology of the public ministry. This is worked out in an essay on 'The Framework of the Gospel Narrative',[1] which is one of the rare serious attempts to refute Karl Ludwig Schmidt's argument that the Marcan order is not chronological. Schmidt and others had called attention to the generalizing summaries (*'Sammelberichte'*) introduced into the Gospel by Mark to hold the narrative together. Dodd now unites all these *'Sammelberichte'* into a continuous text, and defines this as a kerygmatic chronology of the public ministry. Now ingenious though this solution is, it fails, by being a pure conjecture composed of a series of less likely alternatives.

One must first assume that the various *'Sammelberichte'* belonged together as a continuous outline, in the order in which they occur in Mark. But no evidence for this 'original' form in which they circulated is given, and one of the *'Sammelberichte'* is omitted by Dodd himself as unfit for this construction. One must then assume that the order of the reconstructed unit is chronological. But for this assumption one has neither the support of any other kerygmatic text, nor the support of the Gospels. For Dodd is attempting to refute the dominant view since Schmidt of the non-chronological order of the Gospels, and it would clearly be an argument in a circle to assume the chronological order of the Gospels in the argument. Dodd must next maintain that the *'Sammelberichte'* are not, as has been generally supposed,[2] Marcan creations, but rather comprise a pre-Marcan kerygmatic tradition.

[1] This essay of 1932 is reprinted in the volume *New Testament Studies*, 1–11.
[2] The view of Henry J. Cadbury, 'The Summaries in Acts', *The Beginnings of Christianity*, V, 1933, 393, is typical: 'The summaries in the gospels, whether of teaching or healing or both, are not so primitive as the individual stories, and have been largely distilled out of them. They are an indication of an individual author. Their purpose is that of generalizing and of thus filling the lacuna which is felt when a continuous narrative is to be made out of detached scenes. They represent the latest part of Mark, and specially reveal his editorial motives. The later evangelists use these sections of Mark with great freedom. Desiring a still more connected story they show a tendency to repeat and multiply them.'

Dodd's argument here is to the effect that Mark does not actually follow this reconstructed outline; it is assumed that he attempted to do so, and consequently that his failure indicates that the outline was not his own, but came to him from the tradition. However the case for the existence of the conjectured 'outline' really requires for its proof some such objective indication of its existence as would be provided by Mark following it in his narrative. The fact that Mark does not follow the order of the hypothetical outline certainly points to a more obvious inference than the pre-Marcan origin of the hypothetical document: namely, its non-existence. Mark did not follow the outline of the collected '*Sammelberichte*' simply because he was unaware of them as assembled into a chronological outline by Dodd, but knew of them only as he himself presents them: a series of independent generalizing summaries, probably, like the *kerygma* and the Gospels, primarily topical in nature. Dodd's whole thesis with regard to a kerygmatic chronology fails for lack of the confirming evidence required to establish a position which would reverse the course of scholarship, and thus must move against the stream of current views as to the probabilities in the case.[1]

[1]This problem of using an evangelist's presentation of the *kerygma* to prove that his Gospel conforms to an earlier kerygmatic pattern is also being felt increasingly in the case of Luke and the sermons of Acts. When Dodd wrote on the sermons in Acts, de Zwaan had published (in *The Beginnings of Christianity* II, 1922, 30–65) a critical study of Torrey's theory of an Aramaic origin of Acts (*The Composition and Date of Acts,* 1915) and had conceded the existence of Aramaic source material at least behind the speeches. It was upon this that Dodd built (*The Apostolic Preaching,* 20). But scholarly opinion with regard to the speeches of Acts has shifted sharply since the publication in 1949 of Dibelius' 'Die Reden der Apostelgeschichte und die antike Geschichtsschreibung' (*Studies in the Acts of the Apostles,* 1956, 138–85), which is really only a confirmation of Henry J. Cadbury's thesis, 'The Speeches of Acts', *The Beginnings of Christianity* V, 1933, 402–27. Their argument that the composition of the speeches is the work of Luke has gained wide support, and provides the basis for the most recent important commentary, by Ernst Haenchen (*Die Apostelgeschichte,* 1956, e.g. 152 f.; cf. also his essay 'Tradition und Komposition in der Apostelgeschichte,' ZTK LII, 1955, 205–25), as well as for the forthcoming commentary in the *Handbuch zum Neuen Testament* series by Hans Conzelmann. A somewhat extreme example of the new trend is found in C. F. Evans' article on 'The Kerygma' (*JTS,* n.s. VII, 1956, 25–41). Yet it is characteristic of the new period that J. A. T. Robinson, in his soberer answer to Evans ('The Most Primitive Christology of All?' *JTS,* n.s.

B. 'NEW SOURCES'?

The original quest had been brought to an end by the rise of the *kerygma* to the centre of twentieth-century theology. Credit for the centrality of the *kerygma* is largely due, at least in the English-speaking world, to C. H. Dodd. Yet the new spirit, once conjured up, was no longer at the service of the master, and failed to provide him with a new basis for the old quest. Perhaps sensing this situation, the most forthright German attempt to revive the positivistic kind of quest,[1] although carried through by a strong supporter of the *kerygma*,[2] has sought its basis elsewhere. This is the significance of the life of Jesus by Ethelbert Stauffer, which has appeared in English as *Jesus and His Story*, 1960.

VII, 1956, 177–89), assumes the burden of proof for his case that in some instances the sermons contain pre-Lucan tradition. The striking unity in the outlines in the sermons of Acts has led Eduard Schweizer (in conjunction with Hans Conzelmann) to the conclusion that the outline is Luke's contribution ('Zu den Reden der Apostelgeschichte', *TZ* XIII, 1957, 1–11), although he holds that Luke made use of older traditions, especially in the christological section of the sermons (cf. *Erniedrigung und Erhöhung bei Jesus und seinen Nachfolgern*, 1955, sections 6a and 12k). Even when more conservative conclusions along the lines of Dodd are reached, e.g. by Bo Reicke ('A Synopsis of Early Christian Preaching', *The Root of the Vine*, ed. A. Fridrichsen, 1953, 138–41; *Glaube und Leben der Urgemeinde*, 1957, *passim*) and Etienne Trocmé (*Le 'Livre des Actes' et l'histoire*, 1957, 207–14), it is upon the assumption of Lucan composition with use of a traditional form, rather than upon the assumption of early sources incorporated into Acts. Cf. Trocmé, 16: 'Since about 1930 there has been an increasing tendency to abandon the idea of extended sources, and to prefer the hypothesis of the use by the author *ad Theophilum* of isolated accounts, often very brief, which he received either in writing or in oral form. The only source going beyond the range of popular narration in length and content remains the 'diary' of the second part (of Acts). H. W. Beyer, O. Bauernfeind, M. Dibelius, W. L. Knox, W. G. Kümmel, W. Michaelis have defended these ideas, with various nuances.' An even sharper view of the shift in scholarly opinion is given by Haenchen, *Die Apostelgeschichte*, 30–41.

[1]Stauffer explicitly states (*Jesus: Gestalt und Geschichte*, 12) that he proposes to write a 'positivistic' history of Jesus, with facts, chronological sequence, and causal relationships, 'so wie es eigentlich gewesen ist' (*ibid.*, 7; cf. also *KuM*, II, 17).

[2]Cf. his *New Testament Theology*, esp. part three on 'The Creeds of the Primitive Church', and the appendices.

[3]This translation of *Jesus: Gestalt und Geschichte* (1957) was published by SCM Press, London, and Alfred Knopf, New York. Page numbers in the present discussion refer to the German edition.

Initially impressed by the current consensus as to the kerygmatic nature of the Gospels (7), Stauffer bases the possibility of a positivistic quest upon the existence of new sources (8). These are of three kinds.

First are 'indirect' sources: increased knowledge of Palestinian conditions. However this is not basically a new kind of source, but is actually what Ernst Renan a century ago entitled 'the fifth gospel'. And the bulk of this information was collected by Gustav Dalman and Joachim Jeremias toward the opening of the present century, before the modernization of Palestine obscured the tradition of the past. Thus we are not dealing with a new source which has arisen during the last generation, outdating the current position that the quest is impossible, but rather with an old source used by the original quest; and, although one may speak of a quantitative increase of accumulated research, the source itself is less intact now than when the quest came to an end.

Nor is the way in which Stauffer uses this source basically new. He speaks (8) of 'synchronizing' this material with the Gospels to achieve a chronology. But the indirect sources have no chronology of Jesus' life to be synchronized with the Gospels; information about Palestine is merely used (16–18) to identify the season or year fitting Gospel allusions (e.g. harvest in the spring; 15th year of Tiberius as A.D. 28). *Given* the order of the Gospels as chronological, one's knowledge of Palestine could help to set up dates or seasons.[1] But what is here presupposed is precisely what today cannot be presupposed, that the Gospels are in chronological order. What is really synchronized is the Fourth Gospel with the synoptics, much as in the lives of Christ of the nineteenth cen-

[1] The view of Philip Carrington (*The Primitive Christian Calendar; A Study in the Making of the Marcan Gospel* I, 1952), to the effect that the dates one would be setting up are those of the primitive Church's liturgical year, is completely ignored. It is generally agreed that Carrington has gone much too far in carrying through the liturgical implications of the kerygmatic nature of the Gospels. Cf. e.g. T. W. Manson's review, *JTS*, n.s. IV, 1953, 78; Vincent Taylor, *The Life and Ministry of Jesus*, 40–43; and my *Problem of History in Mark*, 1957, 12. Yet it is suprising that Stauffer, who begins by conceding their kerygmatic nature, never even considers this possibility, which could account for any correspondences between Palestinian seasons and Marcan sequence.

tury.[1] One must conclude that the first 'new source' has not helped Stauffer to disprove the present consensus; instead the consensus has been ignored, and the traditional sources, i.e. the Gospels, used in a pre-Schmidt fashion.

The second kind of 'new source' is found in the Jewish (i.e. Rabbinic) polemics against Jesus, which again can hardly be called a 'new source'. Since the Jewish sources have the reverse prejudice to that of the Christian sources, Stauffer assumes (9–10) that one has historical fact when the two agree. The Achilles' heel of this argument is the dependence of Rabbinic allusions to Jesus upon the Christian witness. Stauffer seeks to avoid this difficulty by arguing that if the Jews took over a Christian view, the view must be historically accurate. However this argument would be valid only if one assumed that the Jews were historical critics, rather than polemicists. Where the facts were damaging, they had to deny their historicity or hide them; but where they could easily be given an anti-Christian meaning (as in the case of the virgin birth), they could be left standing. Thus the omission or adoption of Christian views about Jesus in the Rabbinic tradition has no direct bearing upon their historicity.[2]

[1]Compare the review by John J. Vincent (*TZ* XIII, 1957, 366): 'Indeed, the reader is continually confronted with matters of a conjectural or debatable character, not always with justification. This applies particularly to the chronological scheme proposed, which is really the fitting of Synoptic elements into a basically Johannine framework.'
[2]Perhaps recognizing this problem, Stauffer also tries to prove that the Jews had independent sources. Cf. the 'Exkurs', 147 f., and his article 'Messias oder Menschensohn', *Novum Testamentum* I, 1956, 81–103. He asserts that the Jewish polemic cited in the Gospels is obviously independent of Christian influence, since the Gospels had not yet been written. But Stauffer here ignores the pre-Gospel oral tradition, upon which such Jewish polemics could be based. We know that this Jewish polemic was in contact with the oral Christian tradition, for it survived as part of the oral Christian tradition incorporated in the Gospels. And it is antecedently improbable that a polemical tradition would arise apart from contact with those against whom the polemic was directed. Upon this crumbling base Stauffer then builds the thesis that the Jewish tradition up to A.D. 500 was independent of Christian influence, simply because it continues the same 'independent' arguments cited in the Gospels. This he bolsters by observing that some points in the Gospels are ignored in Jewish polemic of the second century (Jesus' claim to the specific title Messiah; the near end of the world; Judas; the trial before Pilate). Now various explanations for these omissions could probably be

Stauffer's third 'new source' is the literature of Jewish apocalypticism (10 f.). However this too is no 'new source', but
rather a source which played a major role in the last phase of the
original quest, culminating in the work of Johannes Weiss and
Albert Schweitzer. One might assume that Stauffer had in mind
the newly discovered Qumran texts. However these have for him
only a negative significance (11). The legalism of Qumran identi-
fies Jesus' legalistic sayings as inauthentic, introduced into the
tradition in the re-Judaizing process carried on by Baptist and
Palestinian Christian forces.

None of Stauffer's 'new sources' actually adds new information
specifically about Jesus. They are merely used to argue for the
historicity of the Christian sources. In this sense they are not so
much new sources for the life of Jesus as new arguments; except
that the arguments are not new. For the 'new sources' are not
used to disprove the kerygmatic nature of the New Testament
sources and their resultant partiality, which Stauffer began (7 f.)
by fully conceding, and then as fully ignores. What *is* new in
Stauffer is the programmatic revival of the positivistic understanding of history. He says the *Verbum Dei incarnatum* is a
nudum factum, and the *quaestio prima* of all theological research is
the reconstruction of the history of Jesus, which can solve among
other things the problem of the absoluteness of Jesus. In his
view of history, as well as in his view of the sources, Stauffer

given (e.g. a Jewish conspiracy of silence—cf. *TWNT* III, 287; V, 696; the
decline of eschatological tension in Judaism and Christianity during the
second century; the dubious apologetic value of the Jewish traitor; unwilling-
ness to allude to Roman jurisdiction over Palestine). But it is probably more
relevant to recall how scanty the *Christian* citations from the Gospels are in
the second century, so that the omission of a few elements by the *Rabbinic*
sources should not be unusual. His argument from silence becomes absurd
when one recalls the amount of source material upon which it is built. To
quote T. W. Manson (*Bulletin of the John Rylands Library* XXVII, 1942–3, 327):
'One point is worth noting: it is that the farther we go back in the Jewish
tradition the more scanty the references to Jesus become. The later Jewish
romances are of some size; the Talmudic references are considerably less in
extent; and, when we come to the Mishnah, there are no direct references
at all. (There are a few possible veiled allusions but nothing that can be
regarded as an absolutely certain reference to Jesus. The passages usually
quoted in this connexion are *Yebamoth*, iv.13; *Aboth*, v.19; *Sanhedrin*, x.1 f.)'

shares the outlook of nineteenth-century liberalism, except that he replaces the critical approach with the conservative principle: *in dubio pro tradito*.[1] His basic weakness is that he has ignored the intervening fifty years, whereas real progress in scholarship, precisely when progress means a shift in direction, comes by means of profound understanding of the valid reasons behind the current position, including the valid reasons it had for rejecting an older view to which we must now in some legitimate sense return. For a return must always be a transformation, accepting the valid arguments levelled against the original position, and accepting the valid achievements of the intervening period.

Whereas Stauffer made much of 'new sources' which are hardly new, there is a source which he does not mention which *is* quite new. Among the Coptic gnostic manuscripts discovered in Egypt at Nag Hammadi in 1945 was a copy of the Gospel of Thomas. This apocryphal gospel is mentioned in patristic allusions,[2] and has been more[3] or less[4] identified with a late and purely fanciful infancy narrative known for some time. However, according to preliminary reports, the Gospel of Thomas from Nag Hammadi[5] actually contains a considerable body of *sayings* of Jesus, some of which are not purely of gnostic invention, but are of a type similar to those in the Synoptics. Thus an increase in the quantity of authentic sayings of Jesus may be reasonably anticipated. Yet the nature of the collection does not seem to be such as to alter basically the kind of history or biography of Jesus which is possible. For we apparently have to do with a collection of individual, unrelated sayings apart from their historical setting or chronological order, and reflecting the gnostic tendencies and outlook of the Jewish Christian Church venerating James. Thus the Gospel of Thomas only adds to the type of material already available from Oxyrhynchus Papyri 1 and 654.

[1] *KuM* II, 22, 27, 28.
[2] Cf. M. R. James, *The Apocryphal New Testament,* 1924, 14–16.
[3] *Ibid.,* 49 ff.
[4] Cf. Edgar Hennecke, *Neutestamentliche Apokryphen,* 2nd ed., 1924, 93 ff.
[5] Published in part in *Neutestamentliche Apokryphen,*[3] ed. W. Schneemelcher, and in full by G. Quispel *et al.* Cf. the latter's preliminary report, 'Unknown Sayings of Jesus', *Universitas* (Quarterly Eng. lang. ed.) II, 1958, 123–30.

C. A NEW VIEW OF THE GOSPELS?

Neither the *kerygma* nor new source material has provided the possibility of a return to the type of quest attempted by the nineteenth century. Nor does such a possibility reside in any general shift in scholarly evaluation of the Gospels.[1] If form criticism served to draw attention to the theology of the Church in the formative period of the oral tradition, scholarship today is concentrating upon the influence of the evangelists' theologies upon the Gospels.[2] And one of the outstanding conclusions of this recent research is that 'Luke the historian' is not a positivistic historian supplying us with the kind of objectively verified chronological, geographical, psychological, developmental information previously assumed, but rather is a theologian of history, presenting us with the construction of history which is meaningful to him. There has been a gradual trend toward recognizing historical aspects of the Fourth Gospel; yet this trend has not led to the conclusion that the Fourth Gospel provides a degree of historical objectivity not found in the synoptics, but at most that it falls within the same general category of 'theology

[1]This needs to be particularly emphasized in view of the ambiguous position of Harald Riesenfeld's pamphlet, *The Gospel and its Beginnings; A Study in the Limits of 'Formgeschichte'*, 1957. The thesis of this work by Sweden's leading New Testament professor is quite clear: the *Sitz im Leben* of the synoptic material was a Christian rabbinate, going back to Jesus himself. Jesus limited his teaching in form and extent to what could be memorized, and had his disciples learn it by heart. Even the narratives of Jesus' deeds were largely formulated by Jesus, with the understandable exception of the passion narrative. Paul memorized this tradition during his fortnight in Jerusalem. Jesus also originated the Johannine meditations. Now this thesis not only matches in undocumented construction the excesses of the form criticism it is intended to disprove, but also does not reflect the actual status of New Testament research at the present time. Hence as the address inaugurating a Congress on 'The Four Gospels in 1957' (held at Oxford in September, 1957) it could lead to an inaccurate view of the current situation on the part of those not familiar with the literature in the field.

[2]Significant recent contributions are: Ernst Fuchs, 'Jesu Selbstzeugnis nach Matthäus 5', *ZTK* LI, 1954, 14–34; Günther Bornkamm, 'Kirche und Enderwartung im Matthäus-Evangelium', *The Background of the New Testament and its Eschatology*, Studies in honour of C. H. Dodd, 1956, 222–60; Willi Marxsen, *Der Evangelist Markus; Studien zur Redaktionsgeschichte des Evangeliums*, 1956; Hans Conzelmann, *Die Mitte der Zeit; Studien zur Theologie des Lukas*, 1954, 2nd ed. 1957, Eng. tr. *The Theology of St. Luke*, 1960.

of history' as do the Synoptics.[1] It must also be recognized that
we have to do with an inverse ratio: the increase in the degree of
historicity attributed to specific points in John has been accompanied by a diminution in the degree of historicity which could
be attributed to the divergent view of the Synoptics.

We do find in current discussion various positive statements
as to the historical reliability of factual material in the Gospels,
not only on the part of writers from whom such might be anticipated,[2] but also from among the Bultmannian group itself.[3]
Although this is a new emphasis, coinciding with the proposal
that the quest be reopened, it is actually not a basic reassessment
of the situation with regard to the sources. For even a generation
ago, when the emphasis was upon the impossibility of the older
kind of quest, the existence of some historical information about
Jesus was conceded by Bultmann.[4] And on the other hand the

[1] Cf. e.g. the appendix in C. H. Dodd's *The Interpretation of the Fourth
Gospel*, 1953: 'Some Considerations upon the Historical Aspect of the Fourth
Gospel', 444–53.

[2] Cf. e.g. Vincent Taylor's list of six reasons why radical scepticism seems
to him excessive, *The Life and Ministry of Jesus*, 36–37, and Joachim Jeremias'
list of five ways in which the danger of modernization can be avoided, 'Der
gegenwärtige Stand der Debatte um das Problem des historischen Jesus',
168 f.

[3] E.g. Käsemann, *ZTK* LI, 1954, 152: 'There are after all pieces in the
synoptic tradition which the historian must simply acknowledge as authentic,
if he wishes to remain a historian.' Similarly Bornkamm, *Jesus of Nazareth*,
10, says he 'cannot share the degree of scepticism' of those who say that
'only a white spot can be indicated . . . on the map of the real history of
Jesus, which was formerly drawn so confidently'.

[4] Cf. e.g. his essay 'The New Approach to the Synoptic Problem', *The
Journal of Religion* VI, 1926, 337–62, esp. 343: 'This conclusion (of form
criticism), however, is not simply a negative one. It has also its positive
significance, since critical analysis has brought out portions which can be
regarded as original traditions.' Further (350): 'There is no reason to doubt
that many genuine utterances attributed to Jesus in these (controversial)
discourses rest back upon accurate historical recollection' (although not the
scenes in which the sayings are placed). Further (357 f.): 'In these (prophetic
and apocalyptic) utterances also it is possible to detect with some probability
genuine words of Jesus, for there can be no doubt that Jesus appeared as
prophet and announcer of the coming Kingdom of God.' Therefore Bultmann could write his *Jesus and the Word* in the same year without putting
'Jesus' in quotation marks, since, as he explains in his introduction, he holds
that in the oldest layer of the tradition we encounter Jesus himself. One often
reads a quotation from this same introduction (e.g. in Vincent Taylor, *ExpT*
LIII, 1941–2, 60; Erik Sjöberg, *Der verborgene Menschensohn in den Evangelien*

modern Bultmannians reopening the quest have not rejected the Bultmannian view of the sources as primarily kerygmatic and only secondarily custodians of factual detail for historians of posterity.[1] The mid-century has brought no basic revolution in our view of the sources, such as characterized the turn of the century. The cause for the reawakened interest in the quest of the historical Jesus lies elsewhere.

D. A NEW CONCEPT OF HISTORY AND THE SELF

If the possibility of resuming the quest lies neither in the *kerygma,* nor in new sources, nor in a new view of the Gospels, such a possibility *has* been latent in the radically different understanding of history and of human existence which distinguishes the present from the quest which ended in failure. 'Historicism' is gone as the ideological core of historiography, and with it is gone the centrality of the chronicle. 'Psychologism' is gone as the ideological core of biography, and with it is gone the centrality of the *curriculum vitae.* Consequently the kind of history and biography at-

---

1955, 214: 'I am of the opinion, that of the life and personality of Jesus we know next to nothing, since the Christian sources have no interest in these things and are overgrown by legend, and since other sources about Jesus do not exist.' But one rarely finds quoted the accompanying statement: 'Little as we know of his life and personality, we know enough of his proclamation to be able to make for ourselves a connected picture of it.' Nor do most readers of that quotation understand the technical sense in which Bultmann there uses the terms 'life' and 'personality'. By a 'life' he means a chronological, developmental biography. It is this in which the sources have no interest, and which we consequently cannot reconstruct. And by 'personality' Bultmann has in mind (cf. *GuV* I, 212 f.) a personality cult, a psychological study, a fascination with Jesus' charm, whereas, as he points out, no great personage in history wishes to be evaluated in such terms, 'for *their* interest was not their personality, but their work'. Thus the well-known quotation is far from a sweeping denial of our ability to know historically about Jesus, and is in harmony with the other positive statements made in the same year.

[1]Cf. e.g. Käsemann, 'Zum Thema der Nichtobjektivierbarkeit', *EvTh* XII, 1952–3, 465: 'Although in fact individual details may reach back to an earlier stage, in principle our Christian history begins with the Easter faith of the disciples. What lies behind, even and especially the historical Jesus, is available today only through reconstruction.' Similarly Bornkamm, *Jesus of Nazareth*, 9: 'To be sure the difficulties in arriving at tolerably assured historical knowledge in the area of the tradition about Jesus have become greater and greater. This has to do with the nature of the sources.'

tempted unsuccessfully for Jesus by the nineteenth century is now seen to be based upon a false understanding of the nature of history and the self. As a result it has become *a completely open question,* as to whether a kind of history or biography of Jesus, consistent with the contemporary view of history and human existence, is possible.

This open question has been obscured during the past generation by the necessary polemics against the impossible and misguided kind of quest. But these polemics have been successful enough for the urgent task of our day no longer to be their mechanical perpetuation, but rather the investigation of the possibility of writing the kind of history or biography of Jesus consistent with our modern understanding of history and human existence.

Nineteenth-century historiography and biography were modelled after the natural sciences, e.g. in their effort to establish causal relationships and to classify the particular in terms of the general. Today it is widely recognized that this method placed a premium upon the admixture of nature in history and man, while largely bypassing the distinctively historical and human, where transcendence, if at all, is to be found. It was primarily Wilhelm Dilthey who introduced the modern period by posing for historiography the 'question about the scientific knowledge of individual persons, the great forms of singular human existence'.[1] Today history is increasingly understood as essentially the unique and creative, whose reality would not *be* apart from the event in which it becomes, and whose truth could not be *known* by Platonic recollection or inference from a rational principle, but only through historical encounter. History is the act of intention, the commitment, the meaning for the participants, behind the external occurrence. In such intention and commitment the self of the participant actualizes itself, and in this act of self-actualization the

[1]'Die Entstehung der Hermeneutik' (1900), *Ges. Schr.* V, 317. Dilthey is becoming increasingly known in the English-speaking world through such works as H. A. Hodges, *Wilhelm Dilthey; An Introduction,* 1944; R. G. Collingwood, *The Idea of History,* 1946, 171–6; Rudolf Bultmann, *History and Eschatology* (Gifford Lectures, 1957), 123 ff.

self is revealed. Hence it is the task of modern historiography to grasp such acts of intention, such commitments, such meaning, such self-actualization; and it is the task of modern biography to lay hold of the selfhood which is therein revealed.

This implication of the modern view of history for biography is only strengthened when one turns to the modern concept of selfhood, and its more direct implications for biography. The self is not simply one's personality, resultant upon (and to be explained by) the various influences and ingredients present in one's heritage and development. Rather selfhood is constituted by commitment to a context, from which commitment one's existence arises. One's empirical *habitus* is the inescapable medium through which the self expresses itself, but is not identical with the self, even when one seems to make it so. For even if one avoids commitment and merely drifts with life's tide, or even if the commitment is merely to hold to one's own past or absolutize one's personality, the resultant selfhood is decisively qualified by the mood of inauthenticity in the one case, or by one or the other form of doctrinaire self-assertion in the other. Consequently it would be a basic misunderstanding of selfhood, to describe the causal relationships and cultural ingredients composing the personality, and assume one had understood the self. Selfhood results from implicit or explicit commitment to a kind of existence, and is to be understood only in terms of that commitment, i.e. by laying hold of the understanding of existence in terms of which the self is constituted.

To be sure, neither the modern view of history nor the modern view of existence involves necessarily a dimension of transcendence. To this extent the classical philologian Ernst Heitsch[1] is correct in sensing that the historian's awareness '*tua res agitur*' is 'nuanced in a particular way' by the New Testament scholar: 'It is a matter of *thy blessedness,* however one may understand this.' The secular historian does not have this particular and narrow concentration of interest, but thinks of '*tua res agitur*' in the comprehensive sense that 'nothing human is foreign to thee'. Yet it is

[1]*ZTK* LIII, 1956, 193.

precisely because of this complete openness to all that is human, that the historian must open himself to encounter with humans who understand their existence as lived out of transcendence.

The first effect of the modern view of history and human existence upon New Testament study was, as we have seen, to focus attention upon the *kerygma* as the New Testament statement of Jesus' history and selfhood. This involved also a positive appraisal of the kerygmatic nature of the Gospels, so that one came to recognize the legitimacy in their procedure of transforming the *ipsissima verba* and brute facts into kerygmatic meaning. Thus the modern approach to history and the self made it easy to emphasize the rarity of unaltered sayings and scenes.

There is however another aspect which is equally true, and yet has not been equally emphasized. If the Church's *kerygma* reduced the quantity of unaltered material, it deserves credit for the quality of the unaltered material. The kind of material which the 'kerygmatizing' process would leave *unaltered* is the kind of material which fits best the needs of research based upon the modern view of history and the self. For the kerygmatic interest of the primitive Church would leave unaltered precisely those sayings and scenes in which Jesus made his intention and understanding of existence most apparent to them. Of course the very fact that the earliest Church could on occasion go on saying it in Jesus' way makes it difficult to be certain that any given saying originated with Jesus rather than in this earliest phase of the Church. And areas where Jesus differed from his first disciples would tend to have disappeared from the tradition. Yet in spite of such difficulties, the 'kerygmatic' quality of the material the primitive Church preserved unaltered means that this material is especially suitable for modern research concerned with encountering the meaning of history and the existential selfhood of persons.

Now that the modern view of history and the self has become formally more analogous to the approach of the *kerygma,* we need no longer consider it disastrous that the chronology and causalities of the public ministry are gone. For we have, for example, in the parables, in the beatitudes and woes, and in the sayings on the kingdom, exorcism, John the Baptist and the law, sufficient insight into Jesus' intention to encounter his historical action, and enough insight into the understanding of existence presupposed in his intention to encounter his selfhood. 'If it is by the finger of God that I cast out demons, then the kingdom of God has come upon you' (Luke 11.20). 'From the days of John the Baptist until now the kingdom of heaven has suffered violence, and men of violence take it by force' (Matt. 11.12). Such authentic sayings, whose exact wording cannot well be reconstructed, whose translation is uncertain, whose out-of-date thought patterns are obvious, are none the less more important historical sources for encountering Jesus' history and person than would be the chronological and psychological material the original quest sought in vain. Consequently Jesus' history and selfhood *are* accessible to modern historiography and biography. And *that* is the crucial significance of Käsemann's remark: 'There are after all pieces in the synoptic tradition which the historian must simply acknowledge as authentic, if he wishes to remain a historian.' *This* kind of quest of the historical Jesus *is* possible.

The positive relevance of the modern view of history and the self to the problem of Jesus has not gone completely undetected. As a matter of fact, Bultmann's *Jesus and the Word* of 1926 was prefaced with a classic statement of the modern view of history, and on this basis he states that his book reflects his own encounter with the historical Jesus, and may mediate an encounter with the historical Jesus on the part of the reader. And Käsemann's brief analysis of the authentic sayings of Jesus[1] concludes that, in spite of the absence of messianic titles, Jesus' understanding of his existence can be deduced from his intentions revealed in his sayings. We have already noted how Fuchs derives his understanding of Jesus' work and person from his conduct and its interpretation in the parables.[2] Similarly Bornkamm[3] recognizes that the possi-

[1] *ZTK* LI, 1954, 144–51.
[2] He also derives Jesus' selfhood from his call for decision (*ZTK* LIII, 1956, 221 f., 227): 'This requirement is simply the echo of that decision which Jesus himself had made. We must understand Jesus' conduct as equally determined by a decision, and consequently we can infer from what he re-

bility of his *Jesus of Nazareth* resides in a new view of history. 'If
the Gospels do not speak of the history of Jesus in the sense of a
reproducible *curriculum vitae* with its experiences and stages, its
outward and inward development, yet they none the less speak of
history as occurrence and event. Of such history the Gospels provide information which is more than abundant.' And his presentation of 'The messianic question'[1] is permeated by the new view
of existence, when he explains that Jesus presented no independent
doctrine of his person precisely because 'the "messianic" aspect of
his being is enclosed *in* his word and act, and in the immediateness
of his historical appearance'. It is consequently not surprising that
Peter Biehl[2] has introduced into the discussion of a new quest a
thematic discussion of the interpretation of history in terms of the
historicity of the self, as found in Martin Heidegger and R. G.
Collingwood.

It is apparent that a new quest of the historical Jesus cannot
be built upon the effort to deny the impossibilities inherent in the
original quest; rather a new quest must be built upon the fact that
the sources *do* make possible a new kind of quest working in terms
of the modern view of history and the self. Whether one wishes to
designate this possible task of historical research a history or life
of Jesus, or whether one prefers to reserve these terms for the
kind of history or life envisaged by the nineteenth century, is not
of crucial importance. The German ability to distinguish between
Historie and *Geschichte* has made it possible, from Bultmann's *Jesus
and the Word* on, to look upon oneself as presenting the history
(*Geschichte*) of Jesus. Such has not been the case with the terms
'life', 'biography', and '*bios*', which continue to be avoided,[3] for

---

quired what he himself did.' 'Believing on Jesus means now in content
repeating Jesus' decision . . . Jesus' person now became the content of
faith.' Cf. also his essay 'Jesus Christus in Person. Zum Problem der Geschichtlichkeit der Offenbarung', *Festschrift Rudolf Bultmann*, 1949, 48–73.
[3]*Jesus of Nazareth*, 24–26.

[1]*Ibid.*, Ch. VIII, esp. 163.   [2]*TR*, n.F. XXIV, 1957–8, 69 ff.
[3]Cf. Käsemann, *ZTK* LI, 1954, 132; Bornkamm, *Jesus of Nazareth*, 9;
and even Stauffer, *Jesus: Gestalt und Geschichte*, 12. It is interesting that Maurice
Goguel entitled the second edition of his *Life of Jesus* merely *Jésus* (1950).

the reason Käsemann gives:[1] 'In a life of Jesus one simply cannot give up outer and inner development.' Since usage determines meaning, it may be that such a nineteenth-century definition of biography is still accurate.[2] But this should not obscure the crucial fact that Jesus' understanding of his existence, his self-hood, and thus in the higher sense his life, is a possible subject of historical research.

[1] *ZTK* LI, 1954, 151.

[2] Cf. Martin Kähler's definition (*Der sogenannte historische Jesus und der geschichtliche, biblische Christus* (1892, reprinted 1953), 23: 'More recent biography seeks its strength in psychological analysis, in demonstrating the quantity of causes and the causal chain out of which the appearance and performance of the person being portrayed has arisen.' The continuation of this definition in the modern period is evident, e.g. in the statement of D. W. Riddle ('Jesus in Modern Research', *The Journal of Religion* XVII, 1937, 177) that we know 'general features' of Jesus, but not such as to write a 'biography', or in the ambiguous statement of C. J. Cadoux ('Is it Possible to Write a Life of Christ?', *ExpT* LIII, 1941–2, 177): 'We do not possess for the life of Jesus anything approaching that knowledge of chronology which is usually deemed necessary for a "biography". . . . I do not concur in the modern view that it is impossible to write a life of Christ.'

IV

THE LEGITIMACY OF A NEW QUEST

A. THE RELEVANCE OF THE THEOLOGICAL QUESTION

The historian may well feel that the *possibility* of a new quest is itself sufficient basis for its *legitimacy,* simply because any possible subject of research is a legitimate topic for the free, inquiring mind. This is certainly true, and one may consequently expect to see from time to time research in this field which is motivated merely by man's insatiable desire to know. However this stimulus would not be such as to provide a concentration of research comparable to that of the original quest, nor could this stimulus produce a new quest which would be a distinctive characteristic of our day, in comparison with other topics where the possibilities of success are much greater. If a new quest of the historical Jesus is to be undertaken on any large scale, it must have some specific impetus in terms of the meaningful concerns of our day, comparable with those which characterized the original quest and its abrupt discontinuation.

The original quest cannot be explained merely in terms of the availability of modern historiography since the eighteenth century. The historical-critical method supplied the means, but not the driving power. An initial impetus had come from the anti-clericalism inherent in much of the enlightenment.[1] But the bulk of the lives of Jesus in the nineteenth century were motivated on the one hand by a desire to overcome the mythological interpretation of David Friedrich Strauss,[2] and on the other hand by

[1] This is the motive of H. S. Reimarus' *Von dem Zweck Jesu und seiner Jünger,* published by Lessing in 1778.

[2] The statement by Willibald Beyschlag (*Das Leben Jesu,* Part I, 3rd ed., 1893, v) is typical: 'Ever since I, as a 21-year-old theological student, let Strauss' *Life of Jesus* with its critique, so superior as to methods and yet so unsatisfying in its conclusions, have its effect upon me, it has been my inner motivation to rebuild for myself in a new, defensible way on scientific grounds the world of faith apparently sinking in these flames.'

the attempt to replace orthodoxy with the Ritschlian system.[1] Similarly the discontinuation of the quest was not due simply to the historical difficulties involved, but rather in great measure to certain theological considerations. It is sometimes assumed that Bultmann's theological position is primarily due to his negative historical conclusions, from which *impasse* he then retreated into Barthianism. However Bultmann has explicitly denied that his move towards Barthianism was due to the negative results of his form criticism.[2] As we have seen, it was Barth himself[3] who called attention to the positive theological significance of radical criticism in eliminating worldly proof as a false support to faith, a position which Bultmann only echoed.[4] Now this positive evaluation of radical criticism in terms of the nature of faith has deep roots in the Marburg tradition out of which both Barth and Bultmann came,[5] but had been radicalized by the discovery of Kierkegaard.[6]

[1] This is in substance the thesis of Albert Schweitzer's *Quest of the Historical Jesus*.

[2] *GuV* I, 101 (1927): 'Wiser persons such as P. Althaus and F. Traub have even detected that I have saved myself from my scepticism (by flight) to Barth and Gogarten. They must excuse me if their wisdom strikes me as comical. I have never felt uncomfortable in my critical radicalism, but instead quite comfortable. But I often have the impression that my conservative colleagues in New Testament feel quite uncomfortable; for I see them always involved in salvage operations. I quietly let it burn; for I see that what is there burning are all the phantasies of the life-of-Jesus-theology, the *Christos kata sarka* itself.'

[3] In the debate with Harnack in *Die Christliche Welt* of 1923, reprinted in Barth's *Theologische Fragen und Antworten*, 1957, 13.

[4] *GuV* I, 4 (1924). Cf. also Bultmann's interpretation of Barth's position, in his review of Barth's *Romans* (*ChrW* XXXVI, 1922, 369): 'Barth rejects this (Ritschlian) answer, not only because he knows that NT research has been largely led to the admission: "Of Jesus' inner life we are hardly able to know anything, as good as nothing." Rather it is because Jesus as a man belongs to psychic, historical reality, to the "world", and we are in no way helped by such psychic, historical perceptibility.'

[5] Cf. e.g. the remark of Martin Rade at the burial of their teacher Wilhelm Herrmann: 'Often it appeared as if research could not turn out radical enough for him.' (*ChrW* XXXVI, 1922, 75). Since Herrmann was primarily concerned with achieving an understanding of faith in terms of encounter rather than of scientific proof, one may detect here the origin of Barth's position. Cf. Barth's lecture, 'Die dogmatische Prinzipienlehre bei Wilhelm Herrmann', 1925, reprinted in Vol. 2 of his *Gesammelte Vorträge, Die Theologie und die Kirche*, 240–84.

[6] Cf. the *Concluding Unscientific Postscript*, Ch. I, 'The Historical Point of

In the case of Bultmann, this theological background was strengthened by his training in the comparative religious school. Here Christianity centres in the cult symbol 'Christ the Lord', whose relation to Jesus of Nazareth was both historically questionable and theologically irrelevant. This position had found its classic expression in Wilhelm Bousset's *Kyrios Christos* of 1913.[1] And Bultmann was sufficiently rooted in this tradition to be entrusted with the editing of the second, posthumous edition, which appeared in the same year as Bultmann's own *Geschichte der synoptischen Tradition*, 1921. Consequently it would be erroneous to see Bultmann's theological position with regard to Jesus as a belated appendix to his historical position; if one were unwilling to concede that the theological and historical factors are inextricably intertwined,[2] then one could equally well argue the priority of the theological. Bultmann himself likes to present his position in terms of Pauline and Johannine theology.

If a new quest of the historical Jesus is to become a significant aspect of theological scholarship during the coming generation, the role which this research will play in the theological thought of our day must be made equally clear. Man's quest for meaningful existence is his highest stimulus to scholarly enquiry; consequently a serious quest of the historical Jesus must have meaning in terms of man's quest for meaningful existence. This does not

---

View,' Para. 1, 'The Holy Scriptures,' esp. 30 ff.: 'While faith has hitherto had a profitable schoolmaster in the existing uncertainty, it would have in the new certainty its most dangerous enemy. For if passion is eliminated, faith no longer exists, and certainty and passion do not go together. . . . For whose sake is it that the proof is sought? Faith does not need it; aye, it must even regard the proof as its enemy.' Already Kierkegaard applied this to the problem of the historical Jesus: 'If the contemporary generation had left nothing behind except the words: "We have believed that in such and such a year God showed himself in the puny form of a servant, taught and lived among us, and then died"—that would be more than enough' (cited by Diem, *Theologie* II, 22).

[1]E.g. (75 of 2nd ed.): 'For the purely historical is really never able to make an impression, but rather only the living present symbol, in which one's own convictions are transfigured and presented.'

[2]Cf. Barth, *Church Dogmatics* I, 2, 493 f.; Ernst Fuchs, 'Probleme der neutestamentlichen Theologie', *VuF, Theol. Jahresbericht* for 1942–6 (1947), 168; Hermann Diem, *Theologie* I, 66.

mean that such a quest should presuppose a given christology,[1] or that it should be oblivious of the peril of modernizing Jesus, this time perhaps in terms of existentialism.[2] It merely means that we must be quite realistic about the day and age in which we live, and its likelihood of producing a new quest. Unless the trend toward regarding the quest of the historical Jesus as theologically irrelevant or even illegitimate is reversed, i.e. unless a new quest becomes for us theologically legitimate and even indispensable, it probably will not enlist the active participation of the strongest intellects and best-equipped specialists, upon whom its success is completely dependent.

B. THE PERMISSIVENESS OF A NEW QUEST

The discussion of the theological propriety of a new quest must naturally begin with the point at which the original quest was seen to be illegitimate. It is illegitimate to dodge the call of the *kerygma* for existential faith in the saving event, by an attempt to provide an objectively verified proof of its historicity. To require an objective legitimization of the saving event prior to faith is to take offence at the offence of Christianity and to perpetuate the unbelieving flight to security. This would signify the reverse of faith, since faith involves the rejection of worldly security as righteousness by works. This line of criticism is a valid identification of the worldliness latent in the 'historicism' and 'psychologism' of the original quest, and must therefore be recognized as a valid theological objection to it.

However it should be equally apparent that this veto upon the original quest does not apply to the modern view of history and historiography which would be presupposed in a new quest. For the objectivity of modern historiography consists precisely in one's openness for the encounter, one's willingness to place one's

[1] This point is well made e.g. by C. J. Cadoux, *ExpT* LIII, 1941–2, 175.

[2] Cf. e.g. Pierre Prigent, 'Les grandes étapes de la vie de Jésus', *Bulletin trimestriel de la Faculté de Théologie protestante de Paris,* 21ème Année, No. 59, March 1958, 28: 'We smile today at the humanistic portrait of Jesus which the nineteenth century painted. But do you think that the same smile will not rise on the lips of those who detect tomorrow, in certain recent works, Jesus the existentialist?'

intentions and views of existence in question, i.e. to learn something basically new about existence and thus to have one's own
existence modified or radically altered. Nor can the end result of
such historical research be a proven *kerygma* dispensing with the
necessity for existential commitment. E.g. from the treatments of
Bultmann, Käsemann, Fuchs and Bornkamm it has not become a
proved fact that God acted in Jesus' intentions or that Jesus is
saviour. At most it has been established that Jesus intended to
confront the hearer inescapably with the God who is near when he
proclaimed 'Repent, for God's reign is near', i.e. that he intended
a historical encounter with himself to be an eschatological encounter with God, and that he consequently understood his existence as that of bringer of eschatological salvation. The historical
Jesus does not legitimize the *kerygma* with a proven divine fact,
but instead confronts us with action and a self which, like the
exorcisms, may be understood either as God's Spirit (Mark 3.29;
Matt. 12.28), or Beelzebub (Mark 3.22), or insanity (Mark 3.21).
The historical Jesus confronts us with existential decision, just
as the *kerygma* does. Consequently it is anachronistic to oppose the
quest today on the assumption that such a quest is designed to
avoid the commitment of faith. That may have been the existential
significance of the original quest, but can hardly be the meaning
of the quest today for a person aware of what is currently known
about historiography and the historical Jesus.

Throughout the generation which emphasized the antithesis
between faith in the *kerygma* and interest in the historical Jesus, it
seems to have been the fact of the Gospels which kept alive some
awareness of the parallelism between the two. For the initial discussion concerning the theological relevance of a new quest has
taken place to a large extent in terms of an exegesis of the evangelists' intention:[1] the evangelists undoubtedly insisted upon the

[1]This approach was anticipated by Karl Ludwig Schmidt, 'Das Christuszeugnis der synoptischen Evangelien', a lecture of 1933–4 published in
Beiheft 2 of *EvTh*, 7–33. Käsemann appropriates it in the decisive section of
his essay 'Das Problem des historischen Jesus' (*ZTK* LI, 1954, 125–53), on
'The Meaning of the Historical in our Gospels', 138–44 (cf. also 133 f.), upon
which the following summary is primarily based. This approach has been

A New Quest of the Historical Jesus

relevance of history for faith. This relevance resided in the identification in the *kerygma* of the humiliated Jesus and the exalted Lord. Now it is characteristic of twentieth-century theology to emphasize one aspect of this identification: the historical Jesus cannot be isolated from the Christ of faith, as the original quest attempted to do. Yet, as the evangelists point out, the other aspect of the identification is equally important: the Christ of faith cannot be separated from the historical Jesus, if we do not wish to find 'a myth in the place of history, a heavenly being in the place of the Nazarene'.

This emphasis upon the humiliation, i.e. the historical in the *kerygma,* is in turn rooted in the eschatological orientation of primitive Christianity. Here again we are accustomed to a one-sided view, in this case with regard to the relation of eschatology and history: the eschatological interpretation placed upon Jesus is largely responsible for the introduction of non-historical material into the Gospels. Yet it is equally true that the eschatological interpretation placed upon Jesus gave to the historical its theological relevance for the evangelists, and thus prevented the disappearance of Jesus into mythology. It is this theological relevance of the historical Jesus for the eschatology of the evangelists which has been examined in some detail:

1. Primitive Christianity experienced Jesus as a unique action of God, creating a situation in which man has an unique opportunity to lay hold of eschatological existence. Revelation was not for them an idea always available to rational reflection, nor was salvation a permanent potentiality of the human spirit. Rather in the last hour God encounters man with a free and gracious opportunity of eschatological existence, a chance which man neglects at his own peril and which therefore places him in ultimate decision. This is what Jesus' earthly life had meant to his followers, and Easter only confirmed this significance. It was this dramatic contingency of the revelation, which found expression in the recording of the concrete history of Jesus in the Gospels.

taken over by Bornkamm, *Jesus of Nazareth*, 24–26, Ernst Fuchs, *Festschrift Rudolf Bultmann*, 54, and Fritz Lieb, *Antwort*, 583.

2. The Fourth Gospel especially is concerned to preserve this awareness of the historicity of revelation, in an environment sufficiently gnostic in its view of religious experience to dissolve Jesus into docetism. In order to dramatize earthly, corporeal existence as the realm of revelation, in order to emphasize the divine condescension of revelation, the Fourth Gospel portrays present religious experience in terms of Jesus' life. The evangelist implements this purpose by drawing attention to the ambiguity, the offence, the hiddenness, which characterized the revelation even in Jesus' life, as if to say: Today it is the same. The Church still remains exposed to the ambiguity of history, the possibility of offence, in spite of having risen with Christ; for the resurrection glory is really the transcendence of his historical existence.

3. By way of contrast the Synoptics betray more of the 'pastness' of Jesus. This may not be due merely to their weaker theological talents, but may indicate a positive insight: although history is determined by present possibilities and decisions, it cannot be dissolved into a series of present situations. Our present possibilities and decisions are determined to a large extent by events of the past, which opened or closed doors for the present. Thus our present situation is part of a larger *kairos,* dating from a past in which the present situation is, so to speak, predestined. In this sense the Christian *kairos* is rooted in the historical Jesus, who is *extra nos,* given prior to faith and determining our present, as the history upon which our existence is constituted.

This clarification of the theological meaning involved in emphasizing Jesus' historicity by writing Gospels does not automatically provide a compelling motivation for a new quest of the historical Jesus. For this meaning expressed in the writing of Gospels was already inherent in the *kerygma,* e.g. in its emphasis upon the humiliation, and can find expression in various forms of Christian experience, e.g. in the experience of Francis of Assisi. Nor does the writing of Gospels form an exact precedent to a quest of the historical Jesus. A quest of the historical Jesus involves an attempt to disengage information about the historical Jesus from its kerygmatic colouring, and thus to mediate an encounter with the historical Jesus distinct from the encounter with the *kerygma*. The Gospels however do not present the historical Jesus in distinction from the *kerygma*, but rather present a kerygmatized history of Jesus.[1]

At the most the discussion of the writing of Gospels presents a parallel in terms of New Testament 'historiography' to the view discussed above, that modern historiography is not in principle a contradiction of faith, but could be used to implement faith's openness to historical encounter. Although the methods of New Testament 'historiography' and modern historiography are quite different, the same or similar kerygmatic motives which produced the one could lead us to a legitimate use of the other. Thus the discussion of the theological meaning of writing Gospels explicates the theological *permissiveness* of a new quest. But the actual *impetus* leading scholarship to make use of this permission resides elsewhere.

C. THE IMPETUS PROVIDED BY DEMYTHOLOGIZING

The debate on demythologizing has been under way since 1941, and it is this movement which is to a large extent responsible for the impetus leading to a new quest of the historical Jesus. As we have seen, it was from among the advocates of demythologizing that the initial proposals of a new quest have come. For the demythologizing of the *kerygma* has drawn attention to a clear alternative inherent in Christian theology:[2] in the process of demythologizing, the objectified language of the *kerygma* loses its own concreteness, and becomes, so to speak, transparent, so that its existential meaning may be grasped. But when the *kerygma* is thus rendered transparent, what is it which then becomes visible

[1] Cf. Heitsch (*ZTK* LIII, 1956, 195): 'To be sure one may say that primitive Christianity did not let the phenomenon of the historical Jesus completely disappear. But does this history (*Historie*) really have relevance for faith? Certainly only as kerygmatized history (in secular language: as history presented in a biased way under the authority of the *kerygma*)! And to be sure, if I accept kerygmatized history as historical, then it simply *must* be relevant to faith, since it was in fact the content of faith which was built into the history.'

[2] Cf., e.g. the Hegelian distinction between the 'Christ-principle' and the 'Christ-person'.

through it? Does one encounter in the *kerygma* a symbolized principle, or interpreted history?

The first alternative conceives of the *kerygma* much as did the comparative-religious school, i.e. as a symbol objectifying a given type of piety, which in turn is the principle or essence of the religion.[1] To be sure this Christian principle would no longer consist in a variant upon Hellenistic mysticism, but would rather be in terms of the historicity of human existence. But in any case the *kerygma* is the objectivation of a truth, not of an event. Or, if one concedes that the witness to an event is essential to the *kerygma*, one must then classify the *kerygma* as essentially mythological, so that 'demythologizing' involves 'dekerygmatizing'.[2]

Now the concept of the *kerygma* as a religious symbol was familiar to Bultmann from his background in the comparative-religious school. Yet it was precisely within his comparative-religious research that he moved away from that basic position. Primitive Christianity is rooted in Jewish eschatology, rather than in Hellenistic mysticism. Consequently it conceives of salvation in terms of the meaning of history, rather than in terms of escape from history. As a result, the myths of the mystery religions were irrelevant for such a Jew as Paul, until he encountered the view that the myth had happened in history. Although Bultmann agrees fully with Bousset that the concepts Paul used in his christology were taken over from the mystery religions rather than handed down from Jesus, he is not misled by this fact into ignoring the decisive role Jesus' historicity plays in the theology of Paul: 'The historical person of Jesus makes Paul's preaching gospel.'[3]

Not only did the coming of the Messiah mean that the eschatological age had dawned, i.e. that eschatological existence was

---

[1]Classical instances of this position are found in Ernst Troeltsch, *Die Bedeutung der Geschichtlichkeit Jesu für den Glauben,* 1911, and Wilhelm Bousset, *Kyrios Christos,* 1913.

[2]This alternative is presented by Fritz Buri, 'Entmythologisierung oder Entkerygmatisierung der Theologie,' *KuM* II, 85–101, and 'Theologie der Existenz,' *KuM* III, 83–91, and by Schubert M. Ogden, 'Bultmann's Project of Demythologization and the Problem of Theology and Philosophy', *The Journal of Religion* XXXVII, 1957, 156–73.

[3]*GuV* I, 202 ff.

possible within history. It also meant that the Pharisaic 'plan of salvation' had simply been by-passed by God, i.e. it meant the replacement of man's presumptive potentiality of self-salvation by the gift of salvation. The Judaism of which Paul had been so proud gave way to his discovery of the present evil aeon, where the egocentric dilemma is such that even the holy law is used self-centredly and only increases man's sin. Thus the eschatological event was God's judgement upon human pride, as well as God's grace giving meaning to human life. Consequently the eschatological event revealed the absence of man's natural possibility of salvation, and thereby only accentuated the indispensability of God's saving intervention. The myth of a mystery religion (or the symbol of the comparative-religious school) could only point out what *ought* to be; as the 'law' of the Hellenistic world it would simply be a new legalism ending like the Jewish law in despair (Rom. 7). Only as witness to God's intervention in history could the myth or symbol be the good news that eschatological existence is possible within history. In this way Bultmann's study of the New Testament *kerygma* compelled him to move beyond the view of it as the objectification of a religious idea, and come to recognize in its 'happened-ness' its essence.[1]

This role in which the *kerygma* played in the thought of Paul finds a parallel in the dilemma confronting modern man, and this parallel has doubtlessly facilitated the appropriation of the Pauline position by the Bultmannian group. This is particularly apparent in the case of Ernst Fuchs: 'We could object that such encounters (*horribile dictu* even with ourselves!) are after all inherent in the meaning of history in general! Why is a Jesus necessary, then, if historical decisions are possible at any time? But how do things stand today (1944) for instance, with the European cultural synthesis demanded by Troeltsch? After all, even in the existence of a single individual, there are often enough decisions which make history. But how do we know that we have thereby achieved the existence that comes from God? And when man becomes conscious of his guilt towards his neighbour, what right has he to

[1]Cf. *Kerygma and Myth,* 14 f., 29 f.

take himself seriously in what he still has ?' 'We are sinners, if we think we are in a position to cope with the guilt of our existence. That is the meaning of the talk about righteousness by works.'[1]

This same sentiment is characteristic enough of our day to have found eloquent expression in W. H. Auden's *Christmas Oratorio*.[2]

> Alone, alone, about a dreadful wood
> Of conscious evil runs a lost mankind,
> Dreading to find its Father lest it find
> The Goodness it has dreaded is not good:
> Alone, alone, about our dreadful wood.
>
> Where is that Law for which we broke our own,
> Where now that Justice for which Flesh resigned
> Her hereditary right to passion, Mind
> His will to absolute power ? Gone. Gone.
> Where is that Law for which we broke our own ?
>
> The Pilgrim Way has led to the Abyss.
> Was it to meet such grinning evidence
> We left our richly odoured ignorance ?
> Was the triumphant answer to be this ?
> The Pilgrim Way has led to the Abyss.
>
> We who must die demand a miracle.
> How could the Eternal do a temporal act,
> The Infinite become a finite fact ?
> Nothing can save us that is possible:
> We who must die demand a miracle.

[1] 'Jesus Christus in Person; Zum Problem der Geschichtlichkeit der Offenbarung', *Festschrift Rudolf Bultmann*, 53, 63. One should note how in this context the problem of Jesus arises. Cf. also Fuchs' comment on Buri's position (*TLZ* LXXXII, 1957, 275): 'It seems to me that one must ask here whether "existence" is given so simply in unhistorical fashion or independent of all history—or whether Buri is not here illuminating an existence which is what it is from the history of Christian reality, i.e. which presupposes that revelation in Jesus which conditions and bears this history.' This latter point is made more clearly in a different context by Peter Biehl (*TR*, n.F. XXIV, 1957–8, 71): 'The traditional question in the philosophy of history, as to the supratemporal meaning of history, which can only be answered when history has reached its end, is a secularized form of Christian cosmic eschatology: similarly the possibility of historical knowledge correctly understood is opened up where Christ is understood by each individual already as the end of history, i.e. where the *historicity of man* comes into view, in Paul and John. Once this possibility is opened up, then it is in principle open also to secular (existentialistic) reflection.'

[2] From *For the Time Being*, Random House, New York, 1944; Faber and Faber, London, 1945, 65 f.

Thus the first assumption as to the purpose of demythologizing, namely that the *kerygma* is a religious symbol objectifying a human potentiality for authentic existence, fails precisely because of what the *kerygma* symbolizes. An unhistorical symbol can hardly symbolize transcendence within history. And the objectification of a human capacity can hardly symbolize man's incapacity before God. Buri is quite correct in recognizing that his alternative is not a demythologization of the *kerygma,* but an elimination of the *kerygma.* But what he has not adequately recognized is that it is not merely an elimination of the 'happened-ness' of the *kerygma,* but thereby also of the existential meaning of the *kerygma.*

Now Bultmann has recognized that the *kerygma* is not a symbol in the same sense as other religious symbols, precisely because of what it symbolizes: as the symbol for transcendence within history it cannot be an unhistorical symbol. Consequently Bultmann emphasizes—in this context at least—that the *kerygma* is a witness to the meaning of Jesus. Thus the other answer to the question 'what the *kerygma* dissolves into' when it is demythologized, is: into the meaning of Jesus of Nazareth. What is encountered when the objectified language of the *kerygma* becomes transparent is Jesus of Nazareth, as the act of God in which transcendence is made a possibility of human existence. The *kerygma* is not the objectification of a new, 'Christian' religious principle, but rather the objectification of a historical encounter with God.[1]

From this position at which Bultmann has arrived it is only one step to the 'post-Bultmannian' recognition that the actual demythologizing which went on within the primitive Church was the 'historicizing' process taking place within the *kerygma* and leading to the writing of Gospels, as has been discussed above. It is simply because Germany's leading exegetes have correctly understood the demythologized meaning of the New Testament *kerygma,* that they have looked through the *kerygma* not directly to a principle

[1]Peter Biehl, 'Welchen Sinn hat es, von "theologischer Ontologie" zu reden?', *ZTK* LIII, 1956, 363, reports: 'On Jan. 30, 1954, in a discussion with Buri before the Basel student body, Bultmann succeeded quite well in showing that his concept of *kerygma* is not a "mythological vestige" in his thought.'

inherent in human nature, but rather to Jesus as the event in which transcendence becomes possible.[1]

D. THE NECESSITY OF A 'NEW QUEST

The theological necessity of a new quest resides in the resultant situation in which theology finds itself today. It is committed to a *kerygma* which locates its saving event in a historical person to whom we have a second avenue of access provided by the rise of scientific historiography since the enlightenment. Apart from this concrete situation, there is no theological necessity for a quest of the historical Jesus, since Jesus can be encountered in the *kerygma*. In this sense faith is not dependent on historiography, which as a matter of fact has been all but non-existent with regard to Jesus during most of the centuries of Christian faith. Yet theological responsibility is in terms of the situation in which we find ourselves placed, and it is an inescapable part of the situation in which we exist that the quest of the historical Jesus has taken place, and in fact has neither proved historically fruitless, nor been brought completely to a halt even among those most opposed to it as an ideological orientation.[2] Thus the problem of the two avenues of

---

[1]Fuchs, *Das Programm der Entmythologisierung*, 1954, 9: 'The encounter with Jesus himself, no more and no less, is the force at work in the so-called demythologizing. Today demythologizing, at least in the area of New Testament scholarship, is encounter with Jesus. I know that I am here going beyond the stage which the debate has reached in recent years. We have made progress.' (Cf. also his concern with the historical Jesus in the context of the quotation on p. 83 above, and his critical position toward Buri, *TLZ* LXXXII, 1957, 275.) Bornkamm, *Jesus of Nazareth*, 23: 'The Gospels signify the *repudiation of myth,* and in so far as its concepts are still or again admitted into the thought of primitive Christian faith, give it once for all the function of interpreting the history of Jesus as the history of God with the world.' Similarly, Käsemann, *ZTK* LIV, 1957, 11: 'Fuchs, G. Bornkamm and I see ourselves compelled to restrict the assertion that Easter founded the Christian *kerygma*; we must enquire as to the meaning of the historical Jesus for faith.'

[2]Both of these latter aspects were recognized by Käsemann in his proposal of a new quest (*ZTK* LI, 1954, 152, 133). Heitsch (*ZTK* LIII, 1956, 195) has most clearly recognized the problem of two avenues of approach to Jesus: 'For here lies a problem which seems to us a decisive problem, namely that rather than one, there are two entities which must be taken from the tradition, both of which have their own requirements and call upon our thinking to take some stand.'

encounter with Jesus must be faced, if we are to theologize realistically in the situation in which we find ourselves.

These two avenues of access to the same person create a situation which has not existed in the Church since the time of the original disciples, who had both their Easter faith and their factual memory of Jesus. They responded to this situation by intuitively explicating their memory until they found in it the *kerygma,* i.e. by 'kerygmatizing' their memory. Thus they largely precluded their situation for the following generations, until we today attempt to disengage their historical information about Jesus from the *kerygma* in terms of which they remembered him. At least to some extent we are thereby returning ourselves to their original situation, which they met by writing the Gospels. It is not their precedent which compels us to express our faith as did they, which in any case would be in many regards impossible. Rather there is an inner logic in the common situation, in which the necessity for a new quest resides. It is this inner logic to which we therefore turn.

The current limitation of New Testament research to the *kerygma* has a significant formal deficiency: it sees Jesus only in terms determined by the Christian encounter, and thus obscures formally the concreteness of his historical reality. If current research upon the New Testament *kerygma* serves to draw attention to the historicity of the proclaimed word of God, as treasure in such earthen vessels as Jewish or Hellenistic thought patterns, research upon Jesus' message would serve formally to draw attention to the flesh of the incarnation. The shock of seeing the all-too-familiar Christ of the traditional gospel within the context of Jewish eschatological sects is comparable to that experienced in portraits, e.g. by Picasso, where half the face is the normal full-face mask, while the other half is cut away, providing insight into what is going on within the head; when one returns to the traditional half of the portrait, one must recall that this conventional view and that 'subliminal' view are together the reality of the person. The formal error of the nineteenth-century quest was to assume that in the Jesus 'according to the flesh' one could see undialectically, unparadoxically, unoffensively Jesus as Lord, whereas one can only see Jesus 'born of a woman, born under the law'. But the formal error of the last generation in eliminating the quest has been to ignore the relevance for the Christian dialectic, paradox, and offence, of seeing Jesus causally bound within the historical reconstruction of first-century Judaism, and yet encountering in him transcendence: 'born of a woman, born under the law, to redeem those who were under the law.'

The *kerygma*, no matter how many mythological concepts it may have made use of in getting its message across, is not proclaiming mythological ideas, but rather the existential meaningfulness of a historical person. Although one may concede that the *kerygma* is not concerned with a Jesus 'according to the flesh', if by this one means a historically proven Lord,[1] it is equally apparent that the *kerygma* is centrally concerned with a Jesus 'in the flesh',[2] in the sense that the heavenly Lord was 'born of a

[1]This is in fact the direction in which the expression moves in contemporary discussion, so that the expression becomes the New Testament equivalent to the technical meaning of the term 'historical Jesus' discussed above. Cf. e.g. Karl Barth, *The Resurrection of the Dead*, 1933, 65 (translation corrected according to Ger. ed. of 1924, 34): 'For what we call the historical Jesus, a Jesus pure and simple, who is not the Lord Jesus, but an earthly phenomenon among others to be objectively discovered, detached from His *Lordship* in the Church of God, apart from the *revelation* given in Jesus to the Church and at first to the apostles—this abstraction was for Paul (and not for him alone) an impossibility. The thought that Jesus should and could be first regarded by himself, in order then to recognize Him as Lord, could at most be for him a painful recollection of his former error. *This* Jesus, who is not the Lord, who is known *after the flesh* (II Cor. 5.16), was in fact the foe whom he persecuted; he no longer knows Him.' Bultmann (*GuV* I, 207) means by 'Christ according to the flesh' 'a phenomenon of the world which one finds given at one's disposal'. From his *Theology of the New Testament* I, 238 f., it is apparent that he, like Barth, expounds II Cor. 5.16 with 'according to the flesh' modifying the verb 'know', so that the epistemological problem is presupposed in the concept 'Christ according to the flesh'. Hence the expression is not used to negate the significance of Jesus' historicity, but rather to negate the importance of the historian's (or disciple's) reconstruction of the historical Jesus. Cf. also Otto Michel, ' "Erkennen dem Fleisch nach" ' (II Kor. 5.16)', *EvTh* XIV, 1954, 22–29.

[2]The expression is itself kerygmatic: I Tim. 3.16; I John 4.2; II John 7; Ignatius, *Smyrn.* 1.2 and *Eph.* 7.2 (*v.l.*). In I Peter 3.18, a kerygmatic text quite parallel with I Tim. 3.16, the expression occurs without the preposition (cf. also 4.1). In Rom. 8.3 the concept of sin is added to that of the flesh, which necessitates the cautious circumlocution 'in the likeness of sinful flesh', which is clearly equivalent to the original expression 'in the flesh' occurring in the same verse. Other equivalent expressions are: 'in the days of his flesh' in

87

woman, born under the law', a historical person. This emphasis in the *kerygma* upon the historicity of Jesus is existentially indispensable, precisely because the *kerygma,* while freeing us from a life 'according to the flesh', proclaims the meaningfulness of life 'in the flesh'.[1]

denies historicity

It is this concern of the *kerygma* for the historicity of Jesus which necessitates a new quest. For how can the indispensable historicity of Jesus be affirmed, while at the same time maintaining the irrelevance of what a historical encounter with him would mean, once this has become a real possibility due to the rise of modern historiography? Such a position cannot fail to lead to the conclusion that the Jesus of the *kerygma* could equally well be only a myth, for one has in fact declared the meaning of his historical person irrelevant. Nor can the requirement of the *kerygma* be met by the observation that Jesus' historicity is beyond question, since one no longer needs to take seriously the unrealistic attacks on his historicity by Bruno Bauer, Albert Kalthoff, Peter Jensen, W. B. Smith, Arthur Drews, P.-L. Couchoud,[2] and, most recently, Communist propaganda.[3] For a myth does not become historical simply by appropriating the name of a historical personage.[4]

Heb. 5.7; the adjective 'fleshy' in Ignatius, *Eph.* 7.2; the genealogical use of 'according to the flesh' in Rom. 1.3; 9.5; Ignatius, *Smyrn.* 1.1 and *Eph.* 20.2; and the expression 'became flesh' in John 1.14 and II *Clem.* 9.5. Note also the emphasis upon Jesus' 'flesh' in Col. 1.22; 2.11; Heb. 10.20; John 6.51–56.

[1] The expression 'in the flesh' is simply an idiom referring to life in the world (II Cor. 10.3; Gal. 2.20; Phil. 1.22). But it comes to be used to point to the *meaningfulness* of life in the world, by drawing the parallel between man's life in the world and Jesus' life in the world: compare Rom. 8.4–13 with 8.3, Col. 1.24 with 1.22, I Peter 4.1, 6 with 3.18.

[2] Cf. the survey of this view since the enlightenment, presented by Goguel, *Jésus,* 39–45. The very absence of recent defences of Jesus' historicity is indicative of the fact that such radically critical positions are untenable and need no longer be taken seriously.

[3] A. P. Gagarin, *Die Entstehung und der Klassencharacter des Christentums,* tr. from the Russian, Dietz Verlag, Berlin, 1955.

[4] Cf. Erik Sjöberg, *Der verborgene Menschensohn in den Evangelien,* 1955, 216: 'Even if Jesus was a historical person, but we could know nothing about this historical person, then the Jesus preached in the Church and portrayed in the Gospels is nevertheless actually a mythological figure. For then he has nothing in common with the Jesus of history, who remains unknown to us, except for the name. Here the New Testament message is much more radically mythological than is presupposed in the contemporary discussion about "demythologizing" the gospel.'

This can be illustrated with regard to the 'cross', whose historicity in the normal sense of the word is not doubted. For in spite of this factuality of the cross, it would none the less be a purely mythological *kerygma*—i.e. a *kerygma* speaking of a selfhood which never existed—if the 'cross' were looked upon only as a physical, biological occurrence, as accidental or involuntary, i.e. as completely distinct from his existential selfhood. Only when preaching the 'cross' means proclaiming Jesus' daily existence as accepting his death and living out of transcendence is it the proclamation of a really historical event.[1] Hence the cross would be misunderstood if its chronological distinctness from the public ministry were looked upon as a basic theological separation from the public ministry, as is all too easy in reaction against Ritschlianism. For example the 'cross' must be interpreted as asserting Jesus' actualization of his message, 'Repent, for God's reign is near'. For this message means a radical break with the present evil aeon, which in turn involves the acceptance of one's own death to and in this world. The revelation that transcendence resides in such a death as this, would be the eschatological saving event in history, just as the Easter *kerygma* claims to be.[2] Yet how can this relation of the 'cross' to his existential selfhood be investigated other than in terms of a new quest of the historical Jesus?

Hence the decisive point with regard to the *kerygma* and history is not whether the *kerygma* preserves detailed historical memories

---

[1] Note the theological concern to speak of Jesus being 'given over' to death or 'betrayed' (both παραδιδόναι), not only by God or Jesus' opponents, but also reflexively by himself: Gal. 2.20; Eph. 5.2., 25; cf. also Gal. 1.4. This view is expressed by the Gospels in their narrative of the journey to Jerusalem, where Jesus teaches the *kerygma* as his intention. In Gethsemane, the Last Supper, and the passion narrative this intention is given dramatic presentation. Käsemann in his 'Kritische Analyse von Phil. 2.5–11' (*ZTK* XLVII, 1950, 313–60) has pointed out that the hymn in Phil. 2.6–11 does not have in view the personality traits of the human, but rather the theological saving acts of the redeemer 'in suprahistorical, mythical framework' (342). Yet he emphasizes (336) that the reflexive pronoun ('emptied himself', 'humbled himself') 'points to Christ's own will and describes the occurrence as his act.' Cf. also Fritz Lieb, *Antwort*, 586.

[2] Cf. Paul Tillich, *Systematic Theology* I, 136: 'The acceptance of the cross, both during his life and at the end of it, is the decisive test of his unity with God, of his complete transparency to the ground of being.'

about Jesus, but rather that the *kerygma* is decidedly an evaluation of the historical person. The *kerygma* does not commit one to assume the historicity of this or that scene in Jesus' life, but it does commit one to a specific understanding of his life. Thus the *kerygma* is largely uninterested in historiography of the nineteenth-century kind, for the *kerygma* does not lie on the level of objectively verifiable fact. But it is decisively interested in historiography of the twentieth-century kind, for the *kerygma* consists in the meaning of a certain historical event, and thus coincides with the goal of modern historiography.

It is because modern historiography mediates an existential encounter with Jesus, an encounter also mediated by the *kerygma,* that modern historiography is of great importance to Christian faith. Käsemann's essay reopening the question of the historical Jesus was instigated[1] by Bultmann's procedure of placing Jesus' message outside primitive Christianity and putting it back into Judaism,[2] as only a presupposition of New Testament theology.[3] Although this classification may be justified and of no great import when limited to the level of the history of ideas, it becomes the crucial issue of the person of Jesus when one recognizes, as does Bultmann in the preface to his *Jesus and the Word,* that it is in the message that one encounters existentially the intention, the understanding of existence constituting the self, and thus the person.[4] If such encounter is not (like the encounter with the *kerygma*) the

[1] *ZTK* LI, 1954, 125 f.
[2] In *Primitive Christianity in its Contemporary Setting* (Ger. ed, 1949).
[3] In his *Theology of the New Testament* I (Ger. ed. 1948).
[4] It is in this sense that one is to understand the crucial importance of Jesus' message throughout Käsemann's basic essay (*ZTK* LI, 1954): 'Most of all, the New Testament itself gives us a right to this question (sc. about the historical Jesus), in so far as the Gospels attribute their *kerygma,* wherever it may come from, to none other than the earthly Jesus, and consequently attribute to him authority which is undeniably exceptional' (133). 'What is of concern to me is the proof that out of the darkness of the history of Jesus, characteristic traits of his proclamation become relatively recognizable, and primitive Christianity combined its own gospel with that proclamation. . . . The question of the historical Jesus is legitimately the question of the continuity of the gospel in the discontinuity of the times and in the variation of the *kerygma.* . . . The gospel is bound to the one who before and after Easter revealed himself to his own as Lord, by placing them before the God who is near and thus setting them in the freedom and responsibility of faith' (152).

eschatological event, i.e. 'Christian', then one must conclude that the message, intention, self, i.e. person, of the historical Jesus is different from what the *kerygma* says his reality is.

This would open the Jesus of the *kerygma* to the same destructive criticism which Bultmann[1] levelled against Barth's 'believer' who does not even know he believes: 'Isn't the *paradox over-stretched?* If faith is separated from every psychic occurrence, if it is beyond the consciousness, is it still anything real at all? Is not all the talk about such faith just speculation, and absurd speculation at that? What is the point of talking about my 'self' which is never my self? What is the point of this faith of which I am not aware, of which I can at most believe that I have it? Is this identity which is claimed between my visible self and my invisible self not in fact a speculation as in gnosticism or anthroposophism, which also speak of relations of my self to higher worlds, relations which are real beyond my consciousness and which are in reality highly indifferent to me? . . . A faith beyond consciousness is after all not the 'impossible possibility', but in *every* sense an 'absurdity'. Is not an incarnation beyond Jesus' historical existence equally an absurdity? Bultmann's procedure of eliminating Jesus' message from primitive Christianity means ultimately that 'Christian faith is understood as faith in the exalted Lord for whom the historical Jesus as such no longer possesses constitutive significance'.[2]

This is not to say that faith hangs upon the question in the history of ideas as to whether Jesus appropriated any specific title available in his culture, or whether he ever spoke as does the *kerygma* in terms of his death and resurrection. But it does mean to say that when the evangelists attribute both to him, they are not merely harmonizing, or changing the *kerygma* into a system invented by Jesus, or betraying their lack of historical ability, but are also stating—admittedly on the externalized level of the history of ideas, and therefore in inadequate form, but nonetheless stating—that the *kerygma* is talking not about a myth, but about the historical existence presupposed in the message of Jesus of Nazareth.

[1]*ChrW* XXXVI, 1922, 358.
[2]Käsemann, *ZTK* LI, 1954, 126.

Although this historical existence could not be proved objectively by any quantity of authentic sayings of Jesus, were they ever so orthodox, yet that historical existence can be encountered historically and understood existentially. And if in the encounter with Jesus one is confronted with the *skandalon* of recognizing in this all-too-human Jewish eschatological message the eternal word of God, and consequently of breaking with the present evil aeon so as to live now out of the grace of God, i.e. if in encountering Jesus one is confronted with the same existential decision as that posed by the *kerygma,* one has proved all that can be proved by a new quest of the historical Jesus: not that the *kerygma* is true, but rather that the existential decision with regard to the *kerygma* is an existential decision with regard to Jesus.

V

THE PROCEDURE OF A NEW QUEST

A. THE PURPOSE AND PROBLEM OF A NEW QUEST

A new quest of the historical Jesus cannot be simply a continuation of the original quest. This fact is most apparent with regard to purpose. For the various factors which motivated the original quest have disappeared with it. The secularization of the West has so advanced that anti-clericalism rarely enlists the best talents of the day. Nor are the Church's opponents likely to be sufficiently embedded in the Christian tradition to be able to participate in biblical scholarship. For specialization has advanced to the degree where membership in the intelligentsia no longer qualifies for participation in the quest of the historical Jesus.[1] Nor can the wish to replace orthodoxy with a more modern theology be a compelling motivation, simply because the hold of orthodoxy upon Western civilization has been so clearly broken that only a Don Quixote would choose to tilt in such a tournament. On the other hand we no longer have an Arthur Drews or P.-L. Couchoud compelling the scholarly world to argue Jesus' historicity. The age of rationalism is past, with its apologetic interest in proving the historicity of the miracle stories by eliminating the miraculous element. For we see that this would merely eliminate the eschatological meaning of Jesus' life to which they in their way attest. Nor do we think that Jesus' personality can be reconstructed as a factor of real relevance to theology today. For apart from the difficulties inherent in the sources, modern man is too rudely awakened to his problems to be lulled by the winsomeness of the charming personality which may (or may not) have been Jesus'. Nor do we hold that an accurate reconstruction of Jesus' teaching can produce an ethical or theological system estab-

[1]This generalization is confirmed by the most recent attempt, that of Robert Graves in *King Jesus*, 1946, and *The Nazarene Gospel Restored*, 1954.

lishing the validity of Christianity. We recognize as basic, that historiography cannot and should not prove a *kerygma* which proclaims
Jesus as *eschatological* event calling for *existential* commitment.

The purpose of a new quest must derive from the factors which
have made such a quest possible and necessary, a generation after
the original purposes had lost their driving force and the original
quest had consequently come to an end. A new quest must be
undertaken because the *kerygma* claims to mediate an existential
encounter with a historical person, Jesus, who can also be encountered through the mediation of modern historiography. A
new quest cannot verify the truth of the *kerygma,* that this person
actually lived out of transcendence and actually makes transcendence available to me in my historical existence. But it can test
whether this kerygmatic understanding of Jesus' existence corresponds to the understanding of existence implicit in Jesus' history,
as encountered through modern historiography. If the *kerygma*'s
identification of *its* understanding of existence with *Jesus'* existence
is valid, then this kerygmatic understanding of existence should
become apparent as the result of modern historical research upon
Jesus. For such research has as a legitimate goal the clarification
of an understanding of existence occurring in history, as a possible
understanding of my existence. Hence the purpose of a new quest
of the historical Jesus would be to test the validity of the *kerygma*'s
identification of *its* understanding of existence with *Jesus'* existence.

As a purposeful undertaking, a new quest of the historical Jesus
would revolve around a central problem area determined by its
purpose. This is not to say that the innumerable detailed problems
involved in research would disappear, or no longer call for solution, but rather that the solution of individual difficulties would
be primarily relevant in terms of implementing the solution of a
focal problem. In the case of a new quest, this focal problem would
consist in using the available source material and current historical
method in such a way as to arrive at an understanding of Jesus'
historical action and existential selfhood, in terms which can be
compared with the *kerygma*.

It is out of this focal problem that the distinctive individual problems of a new quest arise. One seeks an encounter with the whole person, comparable to the totality of interpretation one has in the *kerygma*. Yet the totality of the person is not to be sought in terms of chronological and developmental continuity, which is not only unattainable, but also is a different order of 'wholeness' from that needed to draw a comparison with the *kerygma*. Rather the whole person is reached through encounter with individual sayings and actions in which Jesus' intention and selfhood are latent. Hence the relation of each saying or scene to the whole would be a problem of constant relevance.

The Gospels have in their way met this problem, not only by placing the *kerygma* on Jesus' lips, but also by presenting individual units from the tradition in such a way that the whole gospel becomes visible: At the call of Levi, we hear (Mark 2.17): 'I came not to call the righteous, but sinners'; at the healing of the deaf-mute, we hear (Mark 7.37): 'He has done all things well; he even makes the deaf hear and the dumb speak.' Thus such traditions become kerygmatic, not by appropriating the traditional language of the Church's *kerygma*, but in a distinctive way: They retain a concrete story about Jesus, but expand its horizon until the universal saving significance of the heavenly Lord becomes visible in the earthly Jesus.

Although the evangelists have thus in their way achieved an encounter with the total person in the individual scene, their method cannot be that of a new quest. For although the Church's kerygmatic vocabulary does not necessarily occur in such instances, they are none the less kerygmatized narratives, i.e. they reflect the Easter faith. But the question before us is whether this kerygmatic significance is also visible in an encounter with the total person mediated through modern historiography. Consequently the methods to be followed must be in terms of modern historical methodology.

B. THE CONTINUATION OF THE HISTORICAL-CRITICAL METHOD

In view of the emphasis which has been placed upon distinguishing the new quest from the original quest, it needs to be explicitly stated that a new quest cannot take place without the use of the objective philological, comparative-religious, and social-historical research indispensable for historical knowledge. Contemporary methodology has not discontinued these methods in its new understanding of history, but has merely shifted them more decidedly from ends to means. It is true that the 'explanation' of an event or viewpoint does not consist merely in showing its external causes or identifying the source from which an idea was borrowed. Much of what was once lauded as the 'truth' or 'reality' of history is now mocked by insight into the genetic fallacy. Yet despite all this, knowledge of the external cause or the detection of the source idea is often indispensable for understanding what was involved at the deeper level. Contemporary methodology consists precisely in the combination and interaction of objective analysis and existential openness, i.e. it seeks historical understanding precisely in the simultaneous interaction of phenomenological objectivity and existential 'objectivity'.[1]

[1]Twentieth-century historiography need not surrender the term 'objective' to nineteenth-century historiography. Scholarly objectivity does not reside simply in classifying the particular in categories with wider acceptance than one's own individual view, for such a procedure is blind to the twofold subjectivity residing in the categories of one's school of thought or day and age, and in the pervasive subjectivity of Western rationalism, which blunts true encounter into a merely outward stimulus for one's inner *a priori* faculties. Instead, objectivity resides in a complete openness to what the creative historical event has to say. This involves a willingness to listen for underlying intentions and the understanding of existence they convey, with an ear sharpened by one's own awareness of the problems of human existence, and a willingness to suspend one's own answers and one's own understanding of existence sufficiently to grasp as a real possibility what the other is saying. Thus one's historical involvement, not one's disinterestedness, is the instrument leading to objectivity, and it must be constantly observed that this 'subjective participation' of the historian consists precisely in the potential suspension of his own personal views, for the sake of hearing what the other has to tell him about his existence. Cf. Martin Heidegger *Sein und Zeit*, 1927, 395: 'The historical opening up of the "past" through fateful repetition is so little "subjective" that it alone assures the "objectivity" of history. For the objectivity of a science is primarily determined by whether it can bring to the understanding in uncovered fashion the thematically relevant beings in the basic form of their Being. In no science are the "universal validity" of the standards and the claims of "universality" which the impersonal "one" and its common sense requires, *less* possible criteria of "truth" than in authentic history.' Cf. further Bultmann, 'Ist voraussetzungslose Exegese möglich?', *TZ* XIII, 1957, 414 f.

The use of historical-critical method within modern historio-graphy has met with opposition on theological grounds: would not two methods of studying history necessarily involve two classes of historical reality?[1] But this is not the case. The epistemological situation need no more lead to an ontological inference than it does in modern physics, where complementary methods produce either wave characteristics or particle characteristics, without a resultant inference that one has to do with two distinct sub-atomic worlds.[2] 'Every historical phenomenon is directed toward understanding, and belongs together with this [understanding, which is] its future. . . . The noetic possibility of considering the historical phenomenon with or without its future always prevails in principle within the one historical sphere of reality.'[3] As a matter of fact one can recognize, in the interaction of 'Jesus in the context of dead-and-gone first-century Judaism' and 'Jesus as a possible understanding of my existence', a formal analogy in terms of modern historiography to the *kerygma*'s identification of the Jesus of history with the heavenly Lord.

An analogous criticism has been made with regard to the self-hood of the participating historian: would not two methods of studying history necessarily involve two kinds of self-hood? If selfhood is constituted by the 'world' to which we give ourselves, and the objectified 'world' of critical scholar-ship is different from the existential 'world' of encounter, is not the subject in each case different? Is not the 'I' of an 'I-it' relationship necessarily different from the 'I' of an 'I-thou'

[1]This is the thesis of Heinrich Ott, *Geschichte und Heilsgeschichte in der Theologie Rudolf Bultmanns,* 1955, esp. Ch. I: 'Der doppelte Geschichtsbegriff', 8–57; of Hermann Diem, 'Die Kluft zwischen historischer und theologischer Fragestellung bei Rudolf Bultmann und der Versuch ihrer Überwindung durch das Kerygma', *Theologie* II, 114–26; and of René Marlé, *Bultmann et l'interprétation du Nouveau Testament,* 1956, 32. Cf. the criticisms of this position by Peter Biehl, 'Welchen Sinn hat es, von "theologischer Ontologie" zu reden?' *ZTK* LIII, 1956, 349–72, esp. 369–71 (to Ott), and 'Zur Frage nach dem historischen Jesus', *TR*, n.F. XXIV, 1957–8, 58–61 (to Diem); and by Bultmann, 'In eigener Sache', *TLZ* LXXXII, 1957, 242 (to Marlé). A mediating position is found in Fritz Lieb, ' "Geschichte und Heilsgeschichte in der Theologie Rudolf Bultmanns",' *EvTh* XV, 1955, 507–22 (on Ott's book).

[2]Cf. J. Robert Oppenheimer's Reith Lectures of 1953, *Science and the Common Understanding.*   [3]Peter Biehl, *ZTK* LIII, 1956, 369 f.

relationship ?[1] To this we can begin by answering 'Yes'. But these two selfhoods do not correspond to the 'I' which encounters Jesus through a new quest and the 'I' which encounters him through the *kerygma*. For a new quest would not be confined to purely objective research, but would seek an existential encounter with his person, i.e. an 'I-thou' relation. For it is only where his existence speaks to me, i.e. it is only within an 'I-thou' relation, that the historical Jesus can be compared with the *kerygma*. Nor do I automatically exist in an 'I-thou' relation to the *kerygma*. For I must disengage the kerygmatic fragments from the New Testament before I can encounter them existentially. This is even true of human relations, where a certain degree of instinctive 'historical-critical' study is involved in becoming sufficiently acquainted with a person to lay hold of what his existence means to him. Hence this shifting selfhood is a dialectic inherent in the historicity of human existence.[2]

Nor is the dialectic permanently resolved in the encounter with God; rather it is accentuated by the addition of a further dimension, in which historical encounter becomes revelation. It would be *theologia gloriae,* a sophisticated form of perfectionism, to assume that the Christian is not called upon continually to confront the offence of Christianity when he encounters God. Grace continues to reside in judgement, life in death, revelation in historical ambiguity. It is in this dialectical movement from the old man to the new that one finds the distinctive characteristic of Christian existence (I Cor. 13.8–13), not in some other-worldly immediacy. One need merely recall Luther's definition of Christian existence: '*simul peccator et iustus, semper penitens.*'[3]

---

[1] I am indebted to Carl Michaelson for drawing my attention to this aspect of the problem. Cf. e.g. Martin Buber, *I and Thou,* 1937, 3, 62.

[2] Heidegger, *Sein und Zeit,* 1927, § 76, 'Der existenziale Ursprung der Historie aus der Geschichtlichkeit des Daseins', derives from the historicity of human existence the ontological basis of historical research, with all its detailed specialization, 'even down to its most unpretentious "handwork"' (394).

[3] *Vorlesung über den Römerbrief,* 1515–16, ed. J. Ficker, II, 108. Cf. also the first of the 95 theses: 'Dominus et magister noster Jesus Christus, dicendo: Poenitentiam agite etc. omnem vitam fidelium poenitentiam esse voluit.' Cf. Buber, *op. cit.,* 65: 'No man is pure person and no man pure individuality. None is wholly real and none wholly unreal. Every man lives in the twofold *I*.'

Still another criticism of the continued use of historical-critical method within a theologically relevant quest of the historical Jesus needs to be mentioned. For although it cannot lead to a suspension of that method, it does draw our attention to the basic problem[1] which it presents: 'According to our historical method employed thus far, we have before us apparently authentic material about Jesus in the tradition of the sayings of the Lord, only when the material can be understood neither [as derived] from primitive Christian preaching nor from Judaism. Accordingly, in the surest current way of getting on the track of Jesus' preaching, it is elevated to a methodological presupposition that everything which points toward the post-Easter *kerygma* cannot be considered for Jesus' preaching. Then what significance should the result of this research have for theology?'[2]

This criticism might lead one to suppose that such a method is valid only in terms of the original quest, which largely rejected the *kerygma* as a falsification of Jesus, and consequently set out to distinguish him sharply from that theological perversion. However on closer examination it is apparent that it is not the method, but only the absolutizing of its limited results, which results from the approach of the original quest. The effort to distinguish a historical event from later interpretation is a standard historical procedure, just as it is to question the historicity of such details in the tradition as clearly betray that later interpretation. As a matter of fact it is obvious that at least in some instances—one need think only of the Gospel of John—the *kerygma* was put into the mouth of Jesus by the evangelists. If it is a historical fact that this took place, it is a valid procedure for the historian to attempt to distinguish the 'authentic' from the 'unauthentic'[3] material.

[1]For a discussion of this cf. my article 'The Historical Jesus and the Church's Kerygma', *Religion in Life* XXVI, 1956, 393–409.   [2]Biehl, *op. cit.*, 56.

[3]One may however observe that material regarded as wholly 'unauthentic' in terms of positivistic historiography may not seem nearly as 'unauthentic' in terms of modern historiography. For a saying which Jesus never spoke may well reflect accurately his historical significance, and in this sense be more 'historical' than many irrelevant things Jesus actually said. The hopeless ambiguity of the old term 'unauthentic' can be illustrated in terms of the essay of Erich Dinkler, 'Jesu Wort vom Kreuztragen', *Neutestamentliche Studien für Rudolf Bultmann*, 1954, 110–29. Dinkler maintains that the saying

The use of this method becomes illegitimate only when one fails to recognize its limitation. Although one may well assume that the founder of a sect has something in common with the sect he founds, this method is not able to reach whatever area of overlapping there may have been between Jesus and the Church. The method can affirm the historicity only of that part of Jesus in which he is least 'Christian'. For its 'historicity' depends upon the demonstration that it does not present the Church's view and consequently could not have originated there. Since the new quest of the historical Jesus is primarily concerned with investigating the area in which Jesus and the Church's *kerygma* overlap, the limitation of current methods for identifying historical material is apparent, and the resultant methodological difficulty must be recognized.

C. THE METHODOLOGICAL IMPASSE

The limitation inherent in traditional method cannot be adequately met by a supreme effort to solve the much-belaboured problems which these methodological considerations have rendered all but insoluble. The *kerygma* is to be found *expressis verbis* upon the lips of Jesus in the Gospels. Consequently the most obvious solution as to the relation of Jesus and the *kerygma* has always been that Jesus himself proclaimed the *kerygma:* he claimed

---

about taking up one's cross and following Jesus (Mark 8.34 parr.) is not, as has been usually assumed, 'unauthentic'. It was actually spoken by Jesus—only it did not originally refer to the cross. Instead Jesus was alluding to bearing God's seal or sign, so that one should translate σταυρός as 'Taw' or 'Chi' or 'X', rather than 'cross'. Hence according to Dinkler's interpretation the saying is 'authentic', i.e. spoken by Jesus, but the *meaning* it had for the evangelists and for Christians ever since, i.e. its allusion to Jesus' cross, is 'unauthentic'. Yet even here one must narrow the area of 'unauthenticity'. The traditional interpretation is, according to Dinkler's interpretation, only intellectually 'unauthentic', i.e. Jesus did not mean to refer to crucifixion when he spoke; but existentially the traditional interpretation is seen to be 'authentic', as soon as one recognizes that the existential meaning of the traditional Christian interpretation coincides with the existential meaning of the original saying: 'Surrender of self-assertion before God and surrender of the autonomous freedom which directs itself against God' (128). And in both instances this existential meaning is the meaning of *Jesus'* existence: In the traditional interpretation, I assume my cross as my union with the cross of Christ; in Dinkler's interpretation, I encounter an 'authentic' saying in which Jesus' existential selfhood finds expression.

for himself exalted titles and predicted his death and resurrection, just as the *kerygma* does. However it is precisely these most obviously kerygmatic sayings of Jesus whose historicity has been put indefinitely in suspension by current methodology. For these are the sayings which could most obviously have arisen within the Church as sayings of the heavenly Lord, and then, because of the unity of the heavenly Lord and the earthly Jesus, been automatically handed down with the 'rest' of the sayings of Jesus.

Perhaps the classical instance of such a problem has to do with the title 'Son of Man'. For it is the title to which Jesus most frequently makes claim in the Gospels, and with which the predictions of the passion are usually connected. Now the debate as to whether Jesus actually claimed this title for himself has been going on for nearly a century,[1] and is still not resolved. The classical presentation of the critical position[2] divides the 'Son of Man' sayings into three groups: apocalyptic sayings about the future 'Son of Man'; sayings in which Jesus' passion is spoken of as the passion of the 'Son of Man'; and miscellaneous sayings in which Jesus refers to himself during his public ministry as 'Son of Man'. The first group of apocalyptic sayings are conceded to be authentic, but in them Jesus does not explicitly identify himself with this future 'Son of Man'. The sayings in the second group connected with the passion are considered unauthentic *vaticinia ex eventu*. The sayings of the third group are looked upon as mistranslations of the Aramaic idiom, which means not only 'Son

[1] The history of this debate has been written by Erik Sjöberg, 'Ville Jesus vara Messias?', Bestridandet av Jesu messiasmedvetande i det sista seklets forskning' ('Did Jesus want to be Messiah? The Contesting of Jesus' Messianic Consciousness in the Research of the Last Century'), *Svensk Exegetisk Årsbok* X, 1945, 82–151.

[2] Although the argument is summarized in almost every discussion, perhaps the classic English presentation is that of F. J. Foakes Jackson and Kirsopp Lake in *The Beginnings of Christianity* I, 1920, 368–84. However their tabular presentation is in terms of sources, and the three groups which have become conventional are derived from Jean Héring, *Le royaume de Dieu et sa venue*, 1937, Ch. V, 'Jésus et le "fils de l'homme",' 88–100. This presentation can be found in John Knox, *Christ the Lord,* 1945, 30–44, or Rudolf Bultmann, *Theology of the New Testament* I, 30. The position has been reconfirmed in the unpublished Heidelberg dissertation by Gerhard Iber, *Überlieferungsgeschichtliche Untersuchungen zum Begriff des Menschensohnes im Neuen Testament* (1953), summarized in *TLZ* LXXX, 1955, 115 f.

of Man', but also simply 'man' or 'a man' (i.e. 'I', as in II Cor. 12.2 ff.); or as replacements for an original personal pronoun 'I'.[1] From this analysis of the 'Son of Man' sayings the conclusion is obvious: Jesus did not claim to be the 'Son of Man'. This position has been countered in modern scholarship primarily with the argument that the term 'Son of Man' is not a christological title used by the primitive Church,[2] so could not have been attributed

[1]A. Meyer, *Jesu Muttersprache*, 1896, 95 ff., argued that since 'hahu gabra' ('this man') can be a circumlocution for 'I', the same would be true of 'hahu barnasha'. This interpretation has been generally accepted until Erik Sjöberg ('Litteratur till den bibliska kristologien', *STK* XVI, 1940, 294–305, esp. 299) protested that the conjectured idiom never occurs in Aramaic. Hence he (*Der verborgene Menschensohn in den Evangelien*, 1955, 239, n. 3) presented the alternate thesis: 'If the sayings are original, then one must reckon with the fact that Jesus simply said "I", which was then in the tradition replaced by "Son of Man", as in Matt. 16.13 over against Mark 8.27.' One can observe the effect of this shift upon the classical argument by noting the divergences in the presentations by John Knox from *Christ the Lord*, 1945, 30–44, to *The Death of Christ*, 1958, 86–102. Meanwhile however Matthew Black ('Unsolved New Testament Problems. The "Son of Man" in the Teaching of Jesus', *ExpT* LI, 1948–9, 32–36), while conceding that 'hahu barnasha' never occurs with the meaning 'I', has produced an instance of 'barnasha' meaning 'I' (34, n. 1): 'An exact parallel in Aramaic occurs in *Bereshith Rabba* (ed. J. Theodor, Berlin, 1927, Section 7, Beginning). A certain Rabbi Jacob of Nibburaya had been teaching that fish, as well as other living animals used for food, should be ritually slaughtered. R. Haggai 'heard (of this), and (sent to him) and said, 'Come and receive your punishment' (as a false teacher). R. Jacob replied to him, 'A man (barnash) who has spoken a word according to Torah to be punished. Strange, indeed!' . . ." The reference is unambiguously to the speaker himself.'

[2]The absence of the term from the Church is not as complete as is usually assumed. For in addition to Acts 7.56, the term is reported by Hegesippus (in Eusebius, *Eccl. Hist.* II, 23) as used by James at his martyrdom: 'Why do you ask me about Jesus the Son of Man! He is now sitting in the heavens, on the right hand of the great Power, and is about to come on the clouds of heaven.' Cf. also Hippolytus, *Ref.* 5.26.30; Rev. 1.13; Justin, *Apol.* I, 51.9. Furthermore the title 'Son of Man' occurs in Heb. 2.5 ff., where Ps. 8.4–6 is interpreted christologically, and consequently the original anthropological meaning of the idiom has been replaced by the titular meaning. Jean Héring (*Die biblischen Grundlagen des christlichen Humanismus*, 1946, 5 ff.) has shown that here Ps. 8.4–6 has become a kerygmatic text on the pattern 'pre-existence, humiliation, exaltation', such as occurs in Phil. 2.6–11 and elsewhere. This further draws attention to the role which the concept, if not the term, played in the development of the *kerygma*. Cf. e.g. my 'Formal Analysis of Col. 1.15–20', *JBL* LXXVI, 1957, 270–87, esp. 277–80. Stauffer, *New Testament Theology*, n. 800, calls attention to an undeveloped tendency for the term itself to occur in the *kerygma*. The Pauline concept of the second Adam also belongs in this context. Even those who stress the term's rarity concede that the Church

to Jesus unless he had used it of himself.[1] Now of course there are variations in individual presentations on each side, and occasional concessions of specific points provide a certain fluidity to the debate. Furthermore new insights could conceivably provide new possibilities of solution.[2] Consequently research upon such classical

---

originated the use of the term in at least some of the sayings of Jesus (cf. e.g. Cullmann, *Die Christologie des Neuen Testaments*, 1957, 155-7, and Stauffer, *Novum Testamentum* I, 1956, 82). For the role of the 'Son of Man' in the Johannine tradition cf. Siegfried Schulz, *Untersuchungen zur Menschensohn-Christologie im Johannesevangelium*, 1957. Now Ernst Lohmeyer has clearly gone too far in postulating (*Galiläa und Jerusalem*, 1936, esp. 'Der Menschensohn-Glaube', 68-79) a Galilean branch of the primitive Church with a distinctively 'Son of Man christology' (in distinction to the Jerusalem church's 'Messiah christology'). But on the other hand the varied and imaginative ways in which the term and concept were used by the primitive Church weaken considerably the argument that the Church could not have initiated the identification of Jesus with the Son of Man whose coming he predicted.

[1] This position is well stated e.g. by Oscar Cullmann in his forthcoming *Christology of the New Testament* II, 2.2.

[2] Erik Sjöberg argues that the hiddenness of the 'Son of Man' is a constitutive aspect of the Jewish concept, and on this basis explains both Mark's 'messianic secret' and the absence of any clear identification of himself with the 'Son of Man' on the part of Jesus. Cf. *Der verborgene Menschensohn in den Evangelien*, 1955, and his earlier studies on the problem listed there. The traditional view of the title 'Son of Man' as presenting the 'ideal of humanity', 'the incorporation of the moral ideal in the person of Jesus', had been branded by Baldensperger as a modernization in terms of the humanistic ideal prevalent since the enlightenment. Cf. *Das Selbstbewusstsein Jesu im Lichte der messianischen Hoffnungen seiner Zeit,* and ed., 1892, 178 f. However, when embedded in Jesus' eschatology and applied to his followers (and then, in the moment when all forsake him, to himself), this view has reentered the discussion. Cf. T. W. Manson, *The Teaching of Jesus*, 1931, 211-34; 'The Son of Man in Daniel, Enoch and the Gospels', *Bulletin of the John Rylands Library* XXXII, 1950, 171-93; *The Servant-Messiah*, 1953, 72 ff., 80 f.; C. J. Cadoux, *The Historic Mission of Jesus*, 1941, 90-103; Vincent Taylor, *The Names of Jesus*, 1953, 25-35; *The Life and Ministry of Jesus*, 1955, 77-83. The increasing awareness in Bultmannian circles of the christology implicit in Jesus' eschatology has drawn attention to the incompatibility of this estimate of himself with the imminent expectation of some different 'Son of Man', and hence to the elimination of the whole 'Son of Man' complex from the sayings of Jesus, as a concept both distinct from and even incompatible with that of the kingdom of God. Cf. Käsemann, ZTK LI, 1954, 149 f.; Philipp Vielhauer, 'Gottesreich und Menschensohn in der Verkündigung Jesu', *Festschrift für Günther Dehn,* ed. W. Schneemelcher, 1957, 51-79; Hans Conzelmann, 'Gegenwart und Zukunft in der synoptischen Tradition', *ZTK* LIV, 1957, 281-3; *RGG,* 3rd ed., II, 1958, 668. A somewhat parallel position from a more conservative point of view is found in J. A. T. Robinson's *Jesus and his Coming* (1957), where the historicity of Jesus' prediction of the parousia of the Son of Man is denied, while his public ministry as that of the Son of

problems as the 'Son of Man' can meaningfully be continued. Yet scholarship cannot wait indefinitely on their solution, but must instead seek for completely new ways of bringing Jesus and the *kerygma* into comparison.

D. BASIC PROBLEMS OF A NEW QUEST

The historicity of those sayings of Jesus which are most like the *kerygma* has been put indefinitely in suspense by methodological considerations. Yet there is a considerable body of material about Jesus whose historicity tends to be generally accepted, on the basis of these same methods. This is material whose historicity is conceivable in terms of Jesus' Jewish, Palestinian background, and whose origin in the primitive Church is rendered unlikely by the absence of the distinctive views of the Church, or even by the presence of traits which the Church could tolerate but hardly initiate.[1]

Now the historical material which results from the rigorous application of these current methods is at first sight of little relevance to the purpose and problem of a new quest of the historical Jesus. For the tradition of Jesus' sayings has been purged of all traces of the Church's *kerygma,* and therefore could seem of little value in comparing Jesus with the *kerygma.* However this only appears to be the case; the much more important fact resulting from the application of these methods is that they do succeed in producing a body of material whose historicity seems relatively assured. The very objectivity of the methods used, objective precisely with regard to the *kerygma,* gives to this non-

Man is affirmed. It may prove to be relevant to the 'Son of Man' problem that the Similitudes of Enoch have not yet been identified as belonging to the Qumran library.

[1]These principal considerations are not of course the only tools for investigating the authenticity of material about Jesus, although most of the valid methods in current use merely implement them. For a more detailed presentation of methods cf. Joachim Jeremias, 'Kennzeichen der ipsissima vox Jesu', *Synoptische Studien,* 1953, 86–93, and 'Der gegenwärtige Stand der Debatte um das Problem des historischen Jesus', 168 f.; N. A. Dahl, 'Der historische Jesus als geschichtswissenschaftliches und theologisches Problem', *KuD* I, 1955, 104–32, esp. 114–22; and Franz Mussner, 'Der historische Jesus und der Christus des Glaubens', *BZ,* n.F. I, 1957, 224–52, esp. II: 'Kriterien für den historischen Jesus in den Evangelien', 227–30.

kerygmatic material an importance for comparing the historical Jesus and the *kerygma* which the more kerygmatic sayings never achieved, simply because their relation to the historical Jesus was never fully established. The material whose historicity *has* been established is sufficient in quality and quantity to make a historical encounter with Jesus possible. His action, the intention latent in it, the understanding of existence it implies, and thus his selfhood, can be encountered historically. And this can in turn be compared with the *kerygma*, once the meaning the *kerygma* conveys has begun to shine through the language in which it is communicated.

The kind of individual problems which arise from the purpose and focal problem of the new quest can be illustrated by an examination of some of the comparisons or contrasts which have been made between Jesus and the *kerygma*. Some of the contrasts which have been drawn are so basic that they would if valid tend to obviate even the possibility of a relevant comparison, and deserve therefore to be considered in first place.

One such contrast has been drawn by Käsemann himself:[1] the historical Jesus belongs to the past; only in the *kerygma* does Jesus encounter me in the present. 'In so far as one wishes to speak of a modification of faith before and after Easter, it can only be said that "once" became "once for all", the isolated encounter with Jesus limited by death became that presence of the exalted Lord such as the Fourth Gospel describes.' Yet, methodologically speaking,[2] the historical Jesus I encounter *via* historiography is just as really a possible understanding of my present existence as is the *kerygma* of the New Testament, whose 'contemporaneity' is equally problematic. And as a matter of fact this is the problem with which Käsemann is confronted. A new quest of the historical Jesus 'cannot replace the gospel, since historical remains

[1] *ZTK* LI, 1954, 139. Käsemann further (129) describes the kerygmatizing process as 'delivering the facts of the past from the possibility of being regarded as (just) curiosities and miracles', to which Heitsch (*ZTK* LIII, 1956, 204, n. 1) aptly comments: 'Can we say this? Was Jesus' action and language then [just] a remarkable occurrence whose reproduction would *not* have confronted one with decision (which after all resides in his words!)?'
[2] Cf. e.g. Rudolf Bultmann, 'The Problem of Hermeneutics', *Essays Philosophical and Theological*, 234–61.

are not able to assure us that those fragments of Jesus' message are still relevant to us today and attest to God's present action upon us. Only faith derived from Christian preaching is able to deduce the certainty of God acting upon us even from those fragments, which otherwise would remain only a small part of the history of ideas, and quite a problematic part at that.'[1] However all of this is equally true with regard to the New Testament *kerygma*. This parallel has been obscured by the fact that the term '*kerygma*' can ambiguously refer both to fragments of primitive Christian preaching embedded in the New Testament text, and to the word of God I encounter from the pulpit or in my neighbour today. But if it is true that the *kerygma* of the primitive Christians can become contemporaneous with me in my concrete historical encounters, then, in principle at least, this is equally true of the historical Jesus.

Bornkamm[2] has taken over Käsemann's basic distinction that Jesus' 'once' became at Easter 'once for all', but gives it a somewhat different explanation: The 'once' of 'Jesus' history' becomes the 'once for all' of 'God's history with the world'. Yet 'God's history with the world' is not only the interpretation put upon the history of Jesus by the *kerygma,* but is already the meaning residing in it for Jesus himself. Already for Jesus the 'once' of his historicity was the 'once for all' of God's saving event.[3] For Jesus conceived of his transcendent selfhood as constituted by God's intervention in history. And when one examines the nature of this

---

[1]'Zum Thema der Nichtobjektivierbarkeit', *EvTh* XII, 1952–3, 466.
[2]*Jesus of Nazareth*, 23.
[3]Joachim Jeremias, 'Der gegenwärtige Stand der Debatte um das Problem des historischen Jesus', 170, emphasizes this point even to the extent of minimizing the *kerygma*: 'The gospel of Jesus and the *kerygma* of the primitive Church may not be put on the same level; rather they are related to each other as call and reply. The life, work and death of Jesus, the authoritative word of the one who is able to say Abba, who in God's authority called sinners to his table and who went to the cross as Servant of God, is God's call. The believing witness of the primitive Church, the Spirit-led choir of a thousand tongues, is the reply to God's call. . . . It is effected by God's Spirit, but it does not stand equal to the call. The decisive thing is the call, not the reply.' Here full justice is hardly done to the primitive Church's conviction that their *kerygma* was not merely their Spirit-led reply to God's revelation in Jesus, but rather the heavenly Lord's revelation of himself.

selfhood, one sees that it was not a selfish selfhood, but by its very constitution a selfhood for others.

It was the content of this eschatological selfhood that Jesus should accept his death to the present evil aeon. This is the meaning of the paradoxical saying of Mark 8.35: 'For whoever would save his life will lose it, and whoever loses his life will save it.' In accepting his death he was free from the demonic power of the fear of death, and therein resided his transcendence. Yet the eschatological situation in which he found himself was not yet that of the final blessedness, but rather the 'last hour', in which forgiveness was offered to the penitent. This aspect of the situation was also constitutive of Jesus' selfhood. Hence his selfhood found its positive expression in his role as 'sign' of the eschatological situation to the world. He was finally put to death after persisting in this positive expression of his selfhood. Hence his death was seen as the realization of his eschatological selfhood: free from the demonic power of the fear of death, he was free to give his life for his neighbour. His selfhood was interpreted as *pro nobis* not first by the Church, but already by Jesus himself.

The distinction drawn by Käsemann and Bornkamm is in recognition of the distinctive significance of Easter. And as a matter of fact Easter *was* the revelation of Jesus' transcendent selfhood to his disciples. And yet what was revealed at Easter was the transcendent selfhood of *Jesus,* as the *kerygma* insists; i.e. the Easter experience, even though separated from Jesus' lifetime, was the culmination of their historical encounter with him.[1] And it was the selfhood of Jesus to which they witnessed in the *kerygma.* Hence to maintain that Jesus' transcendent selfhood can be encountered historically is not to minimize Easter, but rather to affirm its indispensable presupposition.

This basic problem as to whether the historical Jesus and the

[1]Cf. Bultmann, *Kerygma and Myth,* 207, n. 1: 'It goes without saying that this Word need not necessarily be uttered at the same moment of time in which it becomes a decisive word for me. It is possible for something I heard yesterday or even thirty years ago to become a decisive word for me now; then it begins (or perhaps begins once more) to be a word spoken to me, and is therefore shown to be a word addressed with reference to my present situation.'

kerygma are sufficiently commensurable to be subject to comparison can be posed in a different way. The *kerygma* proclaims an eschatological saving ·event of cosmic proportions. How can Jesus' understanding of himself, irrespective of what that understanding may have been, be subject to comparison with the *kerygma*'s understanding of the course of history or the condition of the cosmos? Now this would be a valid argument if one understood the self in terms of individual autonomy, so that one's understanding of one's self as subject would be quite distinct from one's understanding of the cosmic or historical situation one confronted as object. When however selfhood is envisaged on the basis of the historicity of the self, i.e. when it is recognized that selfhood is constituted in terms of a 'world' or 'context' to which one gives oneself, then it is apparent that one's understanding of one's self includes an understanding of the 'world' in which one exists.[1] In Jesus' case, his selfhood is eschatological, his life is lived out of transcendence, precisely because he has given himself, to the eschatological situation introduced by John the Baptist. In his baptism he 'repents' of his former selfhood built upon a non-eschatological 'world', and in believing John's message of the eschatological situation assumes the eschatological selfhood which ultimately found expression in the title 'Son of Man'.

Yet this same criticism, that Jesus' understanding of his selfhood is incommensurate with the *kerygma*'s concept of a dramatic shift in the course of history or the cosmos, has been presented in still more radical fashion. Is not this whole assumption that Jesus was concerned with a new selfhood, irrespective of whether it be conceived individualistically or in terms of the historicity of human existence, based upon a false theologizing of the historical Jesus? Was he not much more like a Jewish prophet or Rabbi, concerned basically with moral reform? Did he not simply say what man should do, rather than presenting dramatic views of

[1] Cf. Rudolf Bultmann's remarks to this effect in *Kerygma and Myth*, 203 f. It is clearly not inherent in this approach that theology be reduced to anthropology, as in the case of Bultmann's presentation of Pauline theology (*Theology of the New Testament* I, 190 ff.). Such a consequence has been specifically repudiated by Ernst Käsemann, 'Neutestamentliche Fragen von heute', *ZTK* LIV, 1957, 13 f.

what God has done or will do? It is this contrast between Jesus and the Church which characterized scholarship at the turn of the century.

The sharpest formulation was that of William Wrede:[1] 'The teaching of Jesus is directed entirely to the individual personality. Man is to submit his soul to God and to God's will wholly and without reserve. Hence his preaching is for the most part imperative in character, if not in form. The central point for Paul is a divine and supernatural action manifested as a historical fact, or a complex of divine actions which open to mankind a salvation prepared for man. He who believes these divine acts—the incarnation, death, and resurrection of a divine being—can obtain salvation. This view is the essential point of Paul's religion, and is the solid framework without which his belief would collapse incontinently; was it a continuation or a further development of Jesus' gospel? Where, in this theory, can we find the "gospel" which Paul is said to have "understood". The point which was everything to Paul was nothing to Jesus.'

The very radicality of this quotation draws attention to its basic error: the Jesus of this antithesis is the modernized Jesus of the nineteenth-century biographies. He is of course incompatible with the Paul of the first century (whose unmodern credulity is somewhat overdrawn). For a moral reformer of the Victorian era is quite different from the message of divine salvation proclaimed by an eschatological sect of the Hellenistic world. But once one has come to see Jesus in his first-century context of Jewish eschatology, the basic antithesis tends to disappear. His eschatological message that the kingdom of God is already beginning to break into history is, like Paul's message, 'a divine and superhuman action manifested as a historical fact, or a complex of divine actions which open to mankind a salvation prepared for man': 'If it is by the finger of God that I cast out demons, then the kingdom of God has come upon you' (Luke 11.20). 'Woe to you, Chorazin! woe to you, Bethsaida! for if the mighty works

[1]*Paulus,* 1905. The quotation is the point of departure of Johannes Weiss' *Paul and Jesus,* 1909, 3.

done in you had been done in Tyre and Sidon, they would have repented long ago in sackcloth and ashes' (Matt. 11.21). It is this eschatological action of God in history which Jesus proclaimed, and which reached its final formulation in the *kerygma*.

But even if Jesus was, like the *kerygma*, proclaiming God's dramatic intervention in history, was not its significance for the hearer merely that of a call to moral reform? Had Jesus recognized it as a basic dilemma that man's selfhood has been determined by the 'present evil aeon', and that he is subsequently unable to free himself? Was for him the inbreaking of the kingdom of God the possibility of a 'new being', or was it merely the occasion for a sharpening of one's conscience in view of the impending judgement? Such a distinction has, as a matter of fact, been drawn by Ernst Fuchs:[1] 'What is still lacking for Jesus is now supplemented as a consequence of Jesus' cross: the problem of sin expands to the problem of death as a whole. The question: "What should I do (to become blessed)?" yields to the question, "How do I overcome the impotence, under death's sway, of my existence lost before God?" Rom.7.24.' However in this case it is Bultmann who sees no such distinction, but rather understands Jesus to be here existentially as radical as Paul. If for Paul the *kerygma* means 'pronouncing upon oneself the sentence of death and placing one's confidence not in oneself, but in God who raises the dead (II Cor. 1.9)', then 'it is clear that *these explicit theological trains of thought are not present in Jesus*. But it appears to me to be equally clear that they are only explicating Jesus' thought in definite historical antitheses. . . . What Jesus does not at all express is this, that the only way it is *a priori* at all *possible* for the law to encounter the man who desires to secure himself by his own performance, is by becoming for him the παιδαγωγός. To be sure, no matter how foreign this theological idea may be to Jesus' preaching, factually his message implies it none the less.'[2] Hence Jesus' call for obedience in the eschatological situation logically presupposes an eschatological selfhood.

[1] *Festschrift Rudolf Bultmann*, 55.
[2] *GuV* I, 197 f. Italics by Bultmann.

This survey of basic problems for a new quest has not led to the conclusion that Jesus and the *kerygma* are basically incommensurate, a conclusion which would have made the positive solution of the central problem *a priori* impossible. Rather it has tended to reaffirm the working hypothesis of the new quest: if an encounter with the *kerygma* is an encounter with the meaning of Jesus, then an encounter with Jesus should be an encounter with the meaning of the *kerygma*. However no working hypothesis will long maintain its validity, unless one actually enters with it into the work itself. Therefore at least an initial attempt to work upon the central problem in terms of specific problems should be made.

E. TOWARD THE SOLUTION OF TYPICAL PROBLEMS

The typical formulation of the antithesis between Jesus and Paul around the turn of the century was to the effect that 'Jesus preached the kingdom but Paul preached Christ'. '*The Gospel, as Jesus proclaimed it, has to do with the Father only and not with the Son.*'[1] This distinction has been renewed by Ernst Heitsch as a basic incompatibility between Jesus and the *kerygma*.[2] However here too we may well inquire as to whether we are not dealing with a misunderstanding of both Jesus and the *kerygma*. Certainly Jesus did not teach a christology as the Church did. Yet nothing has been more characteristic of research in the past generation than the growing insight that 'Jesus' call to decision implies a christology'.[3] Nor has anything been more characteristic of recent

[1] Adolf Harnack, *What Is Christianity?* (1900), 144 of the 1957 edition. Italics by Harnack.

[2] *ZTK* LIII, 1956, 208 f.: 'Jesus does not point to his person . . .; rather he immediately retreats behind his words, in order to leave the hearer alone with them. . . . (The primitive Church) concerns itself less with acknowledging a commission to reveal God's will, in confrontation with the substance of Jesus' sentences . . .; rather is it concerned with understanding resurrection and redemption through Jesus as the resurrected Son of God. How little it thereby was able to do justice to the intention of the historical Jesus is nowhere more apparent than in the fact that at times it twisted his intention, and just at the decisive points, in that it intentionally or unintentionally changed the absolute freedom and unprotectedness of man under the claim of God, which Jesus taught, into the freedom merely of the Son of Man.'

[3] Rudolf Bultmann, *Theology of the New Testament* I, 43. Similarly Hans Conzelmann speaks of Jesus' 'indirect' christology (*RGG*, 3rd ed. II, 1958,

research than the gradual detection of early kerygmatic fragments in the New Testament, in which the original eschatological meaning of the christological titles used in the *kerygma* is still apparent, and is clearly distinct from their later metaphysical use: Jesus is 'exalted' to the rank of cosmocrator with the 'name that is above every name, . . . Lord Jesus Christ', in order to subjugate the universe (Phil. 2.9–11);[1] he is made 'Lord and Christ' as the inauguration of eschatological existence at Pentecost (Acts 2.36); in this sense he is 'appointed Son of God according to the Spirit of holiness by the resurrection of the dead' (Rom. 1.4).

Now Heitsch is correct in saying that the Church soon and repeatedly lost sight of the eschatological existence proclaimed originally by the *kerygma*. However this in no way affects its original meaning. If the existential decision originally called for by the *kerygma* corresponds to the existential decision called for by Jesus, then it is apparent that the *kerygma* continues Jesus' message; and if the decision called for by Jesus as well as by the *kerygma* was at the basis of his own selfhood, then it is apparent that his person corresponds to its christology.

---

667 f.): 'Jesus connected the hope of salvation with his person to the extent that he sees the kingdom effective in his acts and understands his preaching as the last word of God before the end.' Cf. also his article *RGG* III, 1959, 361 ff. on 'Jesus Christus'.

[1]Cf. Ernst Käsemann, 'Kritische Analyse von Phil. 2.5–11', *ZTK* XLVII, 1950, 313–60, esp. 335, 340: 'The emphasis can no longer be placed upon the condition of the person of Christ in the different phases of his way, even though individual expressions may tempt us in this direction. When the divine glory of the pre-existent was mentioned, this was done only to bring clearly to light the miracle of the saving act. But in the following lines we always find primary mention of what Jesus did, not of what he was. This is not the least thing that distinguishes New Testament christology from the later viewpoint of the early Church. . . . All these statements are not intended to give a definition of essence in the sense of the christology of the early Church, but rather speak of events in a connected series: he emptied himself, took on the form of a servant, appeared as a being like a man; one could establish the fact that he had become man. It is not a question here of the identity of a person in various phases, but rather of the continuity of a miraculous occurrence.' Similarly Hans Conzelmann, 'Das Urchristentum', *Reformatio*, 1957, 564–73, esp. 568: 'From [Easter] on, faith included the relation to the person of Jesus as the Lord ruling today. Put differently, our relation to God and consequently to the world is constantly determined by him.'

This thesis has been carried through by Ernst Fuchs.[1] The existential meaning of the *kerygma* is still visible in the earliest written source, the Pauline epistles. 'Life means for [Paul] actually the joy which can unite a man with God (cf. also Rom. 14.17), and by "death" he understands the anxiety which must separate a man from God (cf. Rom. 7.24; 8.15, etc.). The man who believes in Jesus as Lord is free for such joy and free from this anxiety' (216). 'Obviously for Paul faith in Jesus comes down to the paradoxical truth that man has found refuge in the very God whom he otherwise flees or would have to flee. . . . It is just in the God of wrath that the God of grace purposes to be found—life in the place where death is, joy in the desert of anxiety. In this sense Paul appealed to the crucified Jesus as the resurrected Lord' (217). Now the crucial question is: 'What does all this have to do with the *historical Jesus?* . . . Is it not easily possible that Paul has placed something quite different or even his own concept of faith in the place of Jesus?'

An answer to this question is sought by Fuchs in a brief study of the historical Jesus: Jesus' parables of God's boundless mercy are in defence of Jesus' own conduct in receiving sinners. 'It is true, he means to say, that God has to be severe. But nevertheless God purposes to be gracious, when a sinful man flees to the very God from whom he would otherwise have to flee in fear of judgement.' Now since one's conduct reflects one's understanding of existence, and Jesus' message corresponds to his conduct, it is legitimate to look also in his message for a commentary on his existence.[2] Since Jesus' message centred in a call for decision, one

---

[1] 'Die Frage nach dem historischen Jesus', *ZTK* LIII, 1956, 210–29.

[2] This methodological point, not mentioned by Fuchs, indicates the way in which Peter Biehl's question (*TR*, n.F. XXIV, 1957–8, 76) to Fuchs is to be answered: 'Wherein is the hermeneutical insight, that from what Jesus requires one can infer what he himself did, based *in terms of existentialistic analysis* ("*existential* begründet")?' Once this point has been clarified, i.e. once it has become permissible to deduce Jesus' decision from the decision for which he called, then it is possible to arrive at his historical factuality in terms of existentialistic analysis. Cf. Martin Heidegger, *Sein und Zeit,* 394: 'If Dasein is "actually" only real in existence, then its "factuality" constitutes itself precisely as a determined casting in terms of some chosen possibility of Being. Then what has "factually" really been, is the existential possibility,

may assume that 'this requirement is simply the echo of the decision which Jesus himself made'. 'So when Jesus directs the sinner
through death to the God of grace he knows that he must suffer.
Committing himself to God's grace, he also commits himself to
suffering. His threats and woes, as well as the severity of his
requirement, all stem from his stern will to suffer. For in all this
Jesus exposes himself to his enemies, although he has the violent
death of the Baptist before his eyes' (224).[1]

Once we have grasped the decision in terms of which Jesus' selfhood is constituted, the repetition of his decision involves the
accepting of his selfhood as one's own. Hence making the decision
for which Jesus called, corresponds to accepting him as Lord.
Jesus confronted his hearer with the question: *'Does God intend us
to feel so free towards him that we appeal directly to him* over against the
well-grounded fear of his judgement which we all have long since
secretly known? That is exactly what the decision of the historical
Jesus affirms. That is why he said to the sinner: "Follow me"
(Mark 2.14), and gave sinners precedence over the righteous.
Thus for the man who hears and follows, Jesus is *indeed* the
Lord' (228).

Now since Paul understands the *kerygma* as calling for basically

---

in which fate, chance, and world-history were actually determined. Since
existence is cast only as actual, historical study will open up the quiet power
of the possible all the more penetratingly, the more simply and concretely it
understands and "merely" presents what has been in the world in terms of its
possibility.'

[1]Fuchs (222) looks upon the death of the Baptist as a significant factor in
constituting Jesus' selfhood: it radicalizes for him the Baptist's call to submit
to judgement. Bultmann (*ZTK* LIV, 1957, 254, n. 1) considers this an attempt
to prove 'through biographical psychological argumentation' Fuchs' correct
insight that 'Jesus' relation to God presupposed suffering from the very beginning' (224). Bultmann's view is: 'Surely one may only say that Jesus'
understanding of God's will contains the possibility of having to suffer.'
However if it is true, as it seems to be (cf. Mark 1.14; Dibelius, *Jesus,* 1951,
57), that the Baptist's death played such a role in Jesus' thought, it would
seem to be a dogmatic limitation of research on the part of Bultmann to
maintain that one may not say it. Hence Heitsch is correct, even if one-sided,
in detecting this theological limitation of historical research on the part of
Bultmann (*ZTK* LIII, 1956, 196–203); and Biehl goes too far in his defence
of Bultmann, in denying that this prejudice ever occurs (*TR,* n.F. XXIV,
1957–8, 62).

the same decision as did the historical Jesus, it would seem that faith in the heavenly Lord not only coincides with commitment to the selfhood of the historical Jesus, but also involves a positive response to his message. 'Certainly (for the Church) repetition of Jesus' decision was something new to the extent that it automatically involved taking a position toward Jesus. Jesus' enemies had seen to that. But it none the less remained the old decision, since it had to claim for itself anew God's will and name. To be sure, Jesus' person now became the content of faith. But that took place completely in the name of the God who had acted upon and in Jesus, and who in the future was to act with Jesus even more, as is apparent in the confessions, their Pauline interpretation, and later the Gospels' (227). It is the role of preaching to restore to christology this existential meaning originally inherent in the *kerygma*.

In this presentation Fuchs has clearly worked out, in terms of the decision constituting selfhood, the basic parallelism between the selfhood of the earthly Jesus and the heavenly Lord, and the correlative parallel between the decision called for by Jesus and the decision called for by the *kerygma*. Thus he has not only contributed a solution to a typical problem of the new quest, but has also illustrated in exemplary fashion the formal pattern in terms of which a solution to the focal problem can be sought.

In view of the current concept of the historicity of the self, it is not surprising that the most characteristic distinction between Jesus and Paul during recent years has been in terms of the differing situations in which they found themselves. Bultmann has made the shift in aeons the decisive factor distinguishing Jesus from Paul: 'Jesus looks into the future, toward the coming reign of God, although to be sure toward the reign *now* coming or dawning. But Paul looks back: *The shift of the aeons has already taken place*. . . . Paul regards what for Jesus was future as present, i.e. a presence which dawned in the past. . . . Since Jesus only stands in anticipation, his message discloses the situation of man in anticipation, while Paul discloses the situation of man receiving, although to be sure also awaiting; for unless one understands awaiting, one cannot understand receiving.'¹ However Bultmann himself² has subsequently modified this position to some extent: 'To be sure it is also true of him, that he knew himself to be between the times. He knows that the power of Satan is at an end, for he saw him fall from heaven like lightning (Luke 10.18); and in the power of God's Spirit he drives out the demons (Matt. 12.28; Luke 11.20), since the reign of Satan is broken already (Mark 3.27). . . . Thus his present activity stands in an "interim".' This recognition of Jesus' present as the interim has led Bornkamm³ to accentuate Jesus' present as the time of salvation, so that Bornkamm's presentation of Jesus' situation comes to equal Bultmann's original presentation of Paul's situation: 'Unmediated presence is always the characteristic of Jesus' words, appearance and action, within a world which . . . had lost the present, since it lived . . . between past and future, between traditions and promises or threats.' Thus the basic distinction between Jesus and Paul in terms of their situations would seem to disappear.

Yet Bultmann⁴ still remains reluctant to interpret Jesus' present as based upon historical encounter: 'This judgement of his about his present comes from his own consciousness of vocation; thus he creates it out of himself; and it is not, as was later the case in his Church, based upon looking back upon an event decisive for him. It is of course possible that the coming of the Baptist and his preaching gave him the initial stimulus as one of the signs of the time which he called upon his hearers to observe (Luke 12.54–56). If Matt. 11.11–14 has at its root a genuine saying of Jesus, and if the passage is not completely created by the Church, then Jesus did in fact see in the coming of the Baptist the shift of the aeons. But he does not look back upon him as the Church later looked back upon Jesus, as the figure through whom the old aeon had been brought to its end and the new aeon had been introduced.'

Here Bultmann attempts to avoid the conclusion that John is

¹*GuV* I, 200 f.
²'Der Mensch zwischen den Zeiten,' *Man in God's Design*, 1953, 44.
³*Jesus of Nazareth*, 75.
⁴'Der Mensch zwischen den Zeiten', *Man in God's Design*, 44.

the shift of the aeons, by casting doubt upon the authenticity of the relevant sayings. However this position is untenable, both because Bultmann himself has not provided sufficient grounds for considering the sayings unauthentic,[1] and because there stand arrayed against him the outstanding treatments of John the Baptist written in the present century.[2] Consequently one must

[1] In *Die Geschichte der synoptischen Tradition* (3rd ed. 1957), 177 f., Bultmann concedes that Matt. 11.7–11a is 'perhaps an authentic saying of Jesus', but doubts the authenticity of the rest. His argument is that both the positive and negative sayings about John could derive from the Church; 'for both points of view were given in the anti-Jewish and anti-Baptist polemic respectively'. Now on form-critical grounds this is certainly a less valid approach than that of Martin Dibelius, who introduced form criticism (*Die urchristliche Überlieferung von Johannes dem Täufer,* 1911) with the position that the Church, in its polemics against the Baptist sect, progressively played down the high positive significance Jesus attributed to the Baptist. Hence the *Sitz im Leben* of the material playing John down is much more apparent than the *Sitz im Leben* of the material speaking highly of John. Bultmann's conjecture that the *Sitz im Leben* of the positive material could be anti-Jewish polemics is nowhere attested in the sources, whereas Dibelius succeeds in documenting the polemical use of the tradition about John in the debate between Christians and Baptists. Hence the authenticity of the positive statements about the Baptist (Bultmann lists: Matt. 11.7–11a, 16–19; 21.32; Mark 11.27–30) cannot on form-critical grounds be put in question to the same degree as that of the negative sayings. Bultmann considers Matt. 11.12 f. as belonging among those sayings in which John is played down, and consequently as clearly unauthentic. For this interpretation he appeals to Goguel (*Au seuil de l'évangile; Jean-Baptiste,* 1928, 65–69), who whoever maintains the authenticity of the saying on the basis of Luke's effort to make some sense out of it: 'The tradition would not have created a declaration whose meaning it had not grasped.' Bultmann further appeals to Hans Windisch, 'Die Sprüche vom Eingehen in das Reich Gottes', *ZNTW* XXVII, 1928, 168 f., who however bases his whole position upon v. 11b, whose unauthenticity is conceded by most (including Bultmann). Windisch does not refer to v. 12. Once v. 12 is removed from the context of v. 11b, the positive exegesis of the saying, and hence its authenticity, become more apparent. Cf. Ernst Percy, *Die Botschaft Jesu,* 1953, 5, 198 ff., and the resultant non-committal position of the 'Ergänzungsheft' to the 3rd ed. of Bultmann's *Geschichte der synoptischen Tradition.*

[2] Martin Dibelius, *Die urchristliche Überlieferung von Johannes dem Täufer,* 1911, concedes the authenticity of: Matt. 11.12 f. (23 ff.: 'the time of John's appearance forms the frontier'); Matt. 21.32 (20 f.: 'Jesus seems to feel himself here in solidarity with John'); Mark 11.27–30 (21 f.: this 'paradigm' is 'a further proof that Jesus felt himself in content kin to John'). Dibelius' position is (29) as a consequence the reverse of that of Bultmann: 'Since the days of John the kingdom of God exists, even though under pressure by the "violent". Therefore the new time begins with John. . . . He introduces the first period in the earthly history of this kingdom. Hence there must at least be recognized in his activity a factor which supported the coming of the kingdom. . . . The Baptist's appearance has a material significance for

simply carry through the logic which Bultmann conceded but hesitated to follow. Since Matt. 11.11–14 has at its root a genuine saying of Jesus, and since the passage is not completely created by the Church, then Jesus did in fact see in the coming of the Baptist the shift of the aeons. Hence to this extent Jesus did look back upon him as the Church later looked back upon Jesus,[1] as the

---

Jesus. . . . In the activity of John, Jesus detected the nearness of the kingdom of God, the kingdom which he felt called to preach.' Nor did Bultmann's subsequent form-critical research alter Dibelius' view. In his *Jesus* (1949), he says (56 f.): 'Jesus (by his baptism) affirmed what he certified later through his praise of the Baptist as the greatest of all those born of women, viz., that in John's call to repentance and in his command to be baptized God had spoken to the nation. . . . We know with certainty only this: the Baptist movement was taken by Jesus as the sign that God's kingdom was in fact drawing near.' Similarly Ernst Lohmeyer, *Das Urchristentum*, I. *Johannes der Täufer*, 1932, 20, 113: 'With the Baptist the dividing-line and the shift of the times is there. The law and the prophets are no longer the last thing which gave meaning and existence to the past. Events are there where formerly prophecies prevailed.' 'What formerly was an object of promise and hope has moved into the stage of action, through and since John.' This is also the view of Carl H. Kraeling, *John the Baptist*, 1951, 156 f.: Matt. 11.12 f. is authentic, and speaks of 'a period of violence that begins with John', who 'stands at the dividing line between the period of anticipation and the period in which the kingdom is present but in conflict.'

[1]There is as a matter of fact in Jesus' 'clear confession' to John (Lohmeyer, *Johannes der Täufer*, 20) something analogous to the Church's *kerygma*. Therefore one may reasonably inquire as to whether there occur in the primitive Church any echoes of Jesus' identification of John as the turning-point. Traces of such a pattern may be found in the tradition Luke uses in Acts 1.22 to support his concept of an apostle, but whose grammatical structure suggests it originated apart from that usage (cf. Dibelius, *Studies in the Acts of the Apostles*, 1956, 111, n. 5, and *Jesus*, 1951, 50). Now this formula seems to be presupposed in Acts 10.37: 'beginning from Galilee after the baptism which John preached', although it has been subordinated to the formula from Luke 23.5: 'beginning from Galilee even to this place (Jerusalem)'. The latter half of the original formula may not have referred to the ascension, as Luke uses it (Acts 1.2), but rather to the ascent to Jerusalem. For the corresponding Aramaic and Syriac expression is used interchangeably of the pilgrimage to Jerusalem and of the ascent of the soul to heaven. Cf. Dirk Plooij, 'The Ascension in the "Western" Textual Tradition', *Mededeelingen der Koninklijke Akademie van Wetenschappen*, Afdeeling Letterkunde, Deel 67, Serie A, No. 2 (39–58), 1929, especially the additional note (55–56) by A. J. Wensinck. This original significance may still be reflected in Luke 9.51: 'when the days drew near for his ascent, he set his face to go to Jerusalem.' Cf. also Mark 10.32; John 2.13; 5.1; 7.8. The possibility of such a Semitic origin of the formula is strengthened when one observes that the opening of the expression ('beginning from . . .') is classified by C. C. Torrey (*The Composition and Date of Acts*, 1916, 6, 23, 25, 36) and de Zwaan (*The Beginnings of Christianity* II,

figure through whom the old aeon had been brought to its end and the new aeon had been introduced. It is therefore not surprising that Käsemann[1] emphasizes: 'The Baptist introduced (the kingdom of God), i.e. brought about the shift of aeons.' Similarly Bornkamm[2] says of the Baptist: 'He is no longer only the proclaimer of the future, but belongs himself already within the time of fulfilled promise', 'the sentinel at the frontier between the aeons'. Consequently the existence of a historical event at the shift in the aeons seems not to be a factor distinguishing Jesus' situation from that of the Church.[3] Both Jesus and the Church look upon their existence in terms of a situation created by divine intervention in the form of historical occurrence.[4]

A further consequence was inherent in Bultmann's original distinction between Jesus and Paul in terms of the shift of the aeons: 'It could also be expressed as follows: Jesus preaches law and promise, Paul preaches the gospel in its relation to law.'[5]

1922, 50) as a clear indication of translation. The emphasis upon the *terminus ad quem* of this formula at Jerusalem and the cross could have led to the disappearance of the *terminus a quo,* just as in the case of the Church's normal *kerygma* the same emphasis upon the cross often led to the disappearance of the *parousia*. Vestiges of the turning-point at John may be preserved in the earliest concept of a Gospel: not only Mark and John begin with the Baptist, but, to whatever extent one can speak with assurance concerning them, also 'Q' and 'Proto-Luke' (note that the famous synchronization of Luke 3.1 f. is for the purpose of dating *John*'s ministry). And traces of John as a turning-point occur in the sermons of Acts (10.37; 13.24 f.) and the credal formula of Ignatius, *Smyrn.* 1.1. John seems in fact to have been the 'beginning of the gospel of Jesus Christ' (Mark 1.1).

[1] *ZTK* LI, 1954, 149.
[2] *Jesus of Nazareth*, 51. It is not clear what Bornkamm has in mind when he states (67) that there is the difference between John and Jesus 'as between the eleventh and the twelfth hour'.
[3] Lieb (*Antwort*, 589, 592) also recognizes this crucial significance of John the Baptist. Biehl (*TR*, n.F. XXIV, 1957–8, 73) refers to this position as too 'rigid', apparently in dependence on Fuchs (*ZTK* LIII, 1956, 221), who does not wish to build his interpretation of Jesus upon Matt. 11.12 f., for: 'We would have to emphasize Jesus' conduct so strongly that one would have to ask oneself why Jesus also teaches anything.' Even if the saying necessarily raised this problem, this would be no valid reason for neglecting such an important saying, whose authenticity Biehl (73) concedes.
[4] Cf. already my argument for a historical *terminus a quo* of the situation presupposed in Jesus' parables: 'Jesus' Understanding of History', *The Journal of Bible and Religion* XXIII, 1955, 17–24.
[5] *GuV* I, 201.

However Käsemann[1] also drew the inference from his own divergent position: 'Jesus did not come to proclaim general religious and moral truths, but rather to say how things stand with the kingdom that has dawned, namely that God has drawn near man in grace and requirement. He brought and lived the freedom of the children of God, who remain children and free only so long as they find in the Father their Lord.' And, as we have already seen, Bultmann[2] has subsequently adopted Fuchs' insight to the effect that Jesus received all at his table, as an action reflecting God's grace: 'The one who proclaims the radical requirement of God at the same time speaks the word of grace.' Jesus' calls for decision with regard to his person in Matt. 11.6, Luke 12.8 f., are, like the *kerygma*'s call for decision with regard to his person, 'at the same time words of promise, of grace: at this very moment the gift of freedom is offered the hearer'. Hence the classical Protestant distinction between law and grace no longer seems necessarily to separate Jesus from the Church's *kerygma*.

It has been an integral part of the method employed in all these comparisons of Jesus and the *kerygma,* that we operate below the terminological level, within the deeper level of meaning. For on the one hand we have recognized that the language of the *kerygma* must become transparent, if an interpretation of Jesus is to be seen through it. And on the other hand the historical Jesus cannot for methodological reasons be approached in terms of sayings where kerygmatic language occurs, but only in terms of sayings diverging from the language of the *kerygma.* However we may well wonder how long an agreement on the deeper level of meaning can continue without at some point producing a similarity of terminology.[3] If it cannot be argued that the Church's *kerygma* provides such a terminological parallel to Jesus' message, because of the uncertainty as to whether he used that language, we must then inquire as to whether the terminology which the historical Jesus is known to have used did not at some

[1] *ZTK* LI, 1954, 151.
[2] 'Allgemeine Wahrheit und christliche Verkündigung', *ZTK* LIV, 254.
[3] Rudolf Otto's *Mysticism East and West* (1932) presents an interesting instance of similar positions producing similar terminology.

point at least come to be used by the primitive Church as synony-
mous with its own *kerygma*. Hence we wish finally to confront
the most typical terminology of Jesus' message with the most
typical formulations of the *kerygma*, to investigate what underlying unity of meaning may exist, and then to inquire as to whether
this meaning ever came to be expressed in a union of the two
terminologies. Thus the solution of *this* typical problem of a new
quest of the historical Jesus should consist in a demonstration
ad oculos.

The essential content of Jesus' message was: 'Repent, for the
kingdom of God is near.' The dramatic future coming of the
kingdom has drawn so near that its coming already looms over
the present, calling for a radical break with the present evil aeon
and an equally radical commitment to God's coming kingdom.
Hence Jesus' thought centres in a call to the present on the basis
of the eschatological event of the near future. He pronounces
divine judgement and blessing, and explains God's other mighty
acts which he does (such as exorcism), on the basis of the nearness
of the kingdom. This call to the present in terms of the nearness
of the kingdom is so central a theme as to produce something
approaching a formal pattern,[1] to which many of Jesus' sayings
conform, and of which the following are typical instances: Matt.
4.17; Luke 6.20 f., 24 f.; Matt. 21.31; 18.3; Luke 11.20.

Repent,	for the kingdom of God is near.
Blessed are you poor,	for yours is the kingdom of God.
Blessed are you that hunger now,	for you shall be satisfied.
Blessed are you that weep now,	for you shall laugh.
But woe to you that are rich,	for you have received your consolation.
Woe to you that are full now,	for you shall hunger.
Woe to you that laugh now,	for you shall mourn and weep.
The tax collectors and the harlots	go into the kingdom of God before you.
Unless you turn and become like children,	you will never enter the kingdom of heaven.

[1] I have tried to show in a forthcoming article, 'The Formal Structure of
Jesus' Message', that this pattern permeates Jesus' whole message and provides the norm for interpreting it. Hence the sayings here compared with the
kerygma are not chosen at random, but are just as central to Jesus' message
as the *kerygma* was to the primitive Church. Cf. Ch. VI of my *Kerygma und
historischer Jesus*, 1960.

If it is by the finger of God that I cast out demons,	then the kingdom of God has come upon you.

Now the essential content of the *kerygma* was equally clear, and therefore also tended to give rise to a pattern of death and resurrection, suffering and glory, humiliation and exaltation.[1]

That Christ died for our sins according to the Scriptures,	And that he was raised on the third day according to the Scriptures,
And that he was buried,	And that he was seen by Cephas, then by the twelve.
That the Christ should suffer these things	And enter into his glory.
The sufferings of Christ	And the subsequent glory.
The one come by the seed of David according to the flesh,	The one appointed Son of God according to the Spirit of holiness by the resurrection of the dead.
Put to death in the flesh	But made alive in the Spirit.
Who was revealed in the flesh,	Vindicated in the Spirit,
Preached in the nations,	Seen by angels,
Believed on in the world,	Taken into glory.[2]

Now when one compares these typical instances of Jesus' message and the Church's *kerygma,* one can readily observe that there is a complete separation in terminology, and even in doctrine: Jesus' message is eschatological, the Church's *kerygma* is christological. Jesus called upon his hearer to break radically with the present evil aeon, and to rebuild his life in commitment to the inbreaking kingdom. Paul called upon his hearer to die and rise with Christ. Yet when one moves beyond such an initial comparison to the deeper level of meaning, the underlying similarity becomes increasingly clear. To break categorically with the present evil aeon is to cut the ground from under one's feet, to open oneself physically to death by breaking with the power structure of an evil society, and to open oneself spiritually to death by renouncing self-seeking as a motivation and giving

[1] I Cor. 15.3–5; Luke 24.26; I Peter 1.11; Rom. 1.3 f.; I Peter 3.18; I Tim. 3.16.

[2] Eduard Schweizer has shown that I Tim. 3.16 is built throughout upon the 'humiliation–exaltation' pattern, but with one irregularity, so as to produce the outline A B B A A B. Cf. *Erniedrigung und Erhöhung bei Jesus und seinen Nachfolgern,* 1955, 63–66, and *TWNT* VI, 414.

oneself radically to the needs of one's neighbour, as one's real freedom and love. To do this because of faith in the inbreaking kingdom is to do it in faith that such total death is ultimately meaningful; in it lies transcendence, resurrection. Thus the deeper meaning of Jesus' message is: in accepting one's death there is life for others; in suffering, there is glory; in submitting to judgement, one finds grace; in accepting one's finitude resides the only transcendence. It is this existential meaning latent in Jesus' message which is constitutive of his selfhood, expresses itself in his action, and is finally codified in the Church's *kerygma*.

The extent to which the *kerygma* continues to reveal the existential meaning of Jesus can be illustrated from an interesting Pauline passage, I Cor. 4.8–13, which describes Christian existence first in eschatological terms such as Jesus used, and then in Paul's more typical language of union with Christ.

Jesus spoke eschatological 'woes' as well as beatitudes, according to the 'Q' version of the 'Sermon on the Mount' (Luke 6.24 f.):

Woe to you that are *rich,* for you have received your consolation.
Woe to you that are *full now,* for you *shall* hunger.
Woe you that that laugh *now,* for you *shall* mourn and weep.

Clearly these woes are pronounced upon those who are out of step with God. They prosper now, in the present evil aeon; hence they will not prosper then, in the kingdom of God. This same eschatological message, in much the same language, is presented by Paul:

Already you are *filled!*
Already you have become *rich!*
Without us you reign!

Here the Corinthians are reproached not simply for prosperity, but rather for prosperity already now, before God's reign comes. They are reigning in the present evil aeon, but Paul longs to reign in God's reign: 'And would that you did reign, so that we might reign with you!' But before God's reign comes, i.e. within the present evil aeon, eschatological existence consists in suffering.

Jesus' beatitudes in the 'Q' version retain also their original eschatological orientation (Luke 6.20–23):

Blessed are you poor, for yours is the *reign* of God.
Blessed are you that *hunger now,* for you *shall* be satisfied.
Blessed are you that weep *now,* for you *shall* laugh.
Blessed are you when men hate you, and when they exclude you and revile you, and cast out your name as evil, on account of the Son of Man. Rejoice in that day, and leap for joy, for behold, your reward is great in heaven.

Now Paul describes himself, in contrast to the Corinthians, in terms of this same eschatological understanding of existence:

For I think that God has exhibited us apostles as last of all, like men sentenced to death; because we have become a spectacle to the world, to angels and to men. We are fools for Christ's sake, but you are wise in Christ. We are weak, but you are strong. You are held in honour, but we in disrepute. *To the present hour* we *hunger* and thirst, we are ill-clad and buffeted and homeless, and we labour, working with our own hands. . . . We have become as the refuse of the world, the offscouring of all things, *until now*.

Thus Paul has described first non-Christian existence, and then Christian existence, in much the same eschatological language which Jesus used. But in the midst of his eschatological description of Christian existence Paul introduces a few phrases which express the existential meaning of the *kerygma*. The identity in existential meaning between Jesus' eschatological message and the Church's *kerygma* could not be made more apparent:

When reviled,   we bless.
When persecuted,   we endure.
When slandered,   we try to conciliate.

As Paul says (v. 17), these are his 'ways in Christ' which he teaches in every church, so that one should not be surprised to find this pattern recurring frequently, e.g. II Cor. 6.8–10:

We are treated as impostors,   and yet are true;
  as unknown,   and yet well known;
  as *dying,*   and behold we *live*;
  as punished,   and yet not killed;
  as sorrowful,   yet always rejoicing;
  as poor,   yet making many rich;
  as having nothing,   and yet possessing everything.

Now this message of life in death is clearly intended as the existential appropriation of the *kerygma,* as becomes increasingly apparent in other instances of this pattern (II Cor. 4.8–12; 1.8 f.; 13.4):

We are afflicted in every way,	but not crushed;
perplexed,	but not driven to despair;
persecuted,	but not forsaken;
struck down,	but not destroyed;
always carrying in the body the *death of Jesus*,	so that the *life of Jesus* may also be manifested in our bodies.
For while we live we are always being given up to *death for Jesus' sake*,	so that the *life of Jesus* may be manifested in our mortal flesh.
So *death* is at work in us,	but *life* in you.
We do not want you to be ignorant, brethren, of the affliction we experienced in Asia; for we were so utterly, unbearably crushed that we despaired of life itself. Why, we felt that we had received the sentence of *death*;	but that was to make us rely not on ourselves, but on God who *raises* the dead.
He was crucified in *weakness*,	but *lives by the power of God.*
We are *weak in him*,	but shall *live with him by the power of God* toward you.

Thus Paul's description of his Christian existence is rooted in the *kerygma*, in which Jesus' transcendent selfhood is proclaimed. It is no coincidence that it is precisely in this context (I Cor. 4.16) that Paul can call upon the Corinthians to 'be imitators of me', for the implication is clear: 'Be imitators of me, as I am of Christ' (I Cor. 11.1). Paul's transcendent existence is one with the selfhood of Jesus proclaimed by the *kerygma*.

It is in this sense that one can detect the existential significance of Paul's mystic language: 'Christ is our life' (Col. 3.4). 'It is no longer I who live, but Christ who lives in me' (Gal. 2.20). Our 'life' which is 'hid with Christ in God' (Col. 3.3) is the transcendent selfhood created by Jesus, and made available to us by him. In this way the line of continuity from the historical Jesus to the Second Adam of Pauline speculation is apparent. And, although we today no longer use these speculative categories, the selfhood of Jesus is equally available to us—apparently both *via* historical research and *via* the *kerygma*—as a possible understanding of our existence.

INDEX OF AUTHORS